ENDLESS WAR

**How We Got Involved in Central America—
and What Can Be Done**

ENDLESS WAR

How We Got Involved in Central America— and What Can Be Done

JAMES CHACE

VINTAGE BOOKS

A Division of Random House · New York

A VINTAGE ORIGINAL, September 1984
FIRST EDITION
Copyright © 1984 by Swain Enterprises

Portions of this book first appeared
in the *New York Review of Books*.

Cover photograph by Susan Meiselas/Magnum

Library of Congress Cataloging in Publication Data
Chace, James.
Endless war.
"A Vintage original"—T.p. verso.
1. Central America—Politics and government—1979–
2. Central America—Foreign relations—United States.
3. United States—Foreign relations—Central America.
I. Title
F1439.5.C48 1984   972.8′052   84–48004
ISBN 0–394–72779–7

for Robert Silvers

ACKNOWLEDGMENTS

I have dedicated this book to Robert Silvers, who encouraged me to travel to Central America and Cuba and to write about American policy in the region. I am also indebted to my editor, Jason Epstein, for his wise advice in helping me prepare this work for publication. For his extraordinary efforts in making it possible for me to publish this manuscript, I am most deeply grateful to Caleb Carr.

For their views of aspects of a work in progress, I wish to thank Susan Kaufman Purcell and Jeffrey Garten. Once again I am particularly beholden to Mae Benett for her support and to Grace Darling for her encouragement. Mark Uhlig was a tireless and invaluable companion throughout my travels in the region, and Christopher Dickey proved a shrewd and sensitive observer of events there.

And finally, most of all I thank Susan Chace, my wife, for her understanding of what is important.

PART
1

1

The American army base in Honduras is set up in a narrow valley about two hours by jeep from the capital of Tegucigalpa. The narrow roads wind along the rims of hills like those below San Francisco on the route to Santa Cruz—sudden sharp landfalls to green meadows below. Because the Joint Task Force is supposed to be in Honduras for only a few months, the 41st Combat Support Hospital is made up of a series of connecting tents. Air conditioners are cut into the canvas. At headquarters company the men sleep in well-appointed tents with the flaps open at the sides to let the warm air sift through. The aircraft of the 101st Aviation Battalion kick up clouds as the planes and helicopters take off from the dusty runways. The U.S. troops—about 3,500 of them in the fall of 1983—have been here on joint maneuvers with the Honduran army, which has about 12,500 troops. Neighboring Nicaragua, with its army of 25,000 regulars (the largest in the region), is wary of the military exercises being conducted near its borders. At another base, the Regional Military Training Center (ostensibly under the control of the Honduran government), the United States is training Salvadoran and Honduran troops, and Guatemalans, if they will come. Yet despite this impressive display of military might, the purpose behind it all is far from clear, both to Americans at home and to our soldiers in Honduras. As a young officer said to me, "And now I've got a question for you. What am I doing here?"

What are we doing there? It is a question that requires and deserves an answer, given the long history of suffering in Central America and the harsh debates that the U.S. presence in that region has caused from time to time in our own country. Many answers have been offered over the years—strategic, economic, ideological—and the Reagan Administration has offered its own: the threat of Soviet-Cuban expansionism in the region and the need for the United States to demonstrate its "credibility" as a great power to control events within its own sphere of influence. In addition, the Administration has sought to portray these answers as fresh, in order to justify increased military expenditure and heightened diplomatic intransigence. In fact, the Reagan Administration's present Central American policy is in no way a "new" answer to a "recent" crisis—but simply the latest variation on a policy more than a hundred and fifty years old. The conflict in Central America did not begin five or even seventy-five years ago; it began early in the last century, and our involvement in it has been more or less constant all along.

What is the American policy that has helped produce this dismal result, this seemingly endless war? What, if anything, does it have to do with the improvement of the economies of Central America, or the encouragement of democracy there, or even the creation of true stability in the region? To attain such goals, Washington would have had to confront the real nature and needs of the five Central American states (Guatemala, El Salvador, Honduras, Nicaragua and Costa Rica). Our policy in Central America has never derived from such considerations, however, but rather from fear. Two fears, to be precise.

Since the enunciation of the Monroe Doctrine in 1823, two separate but interrelated anxieties have dominated U.S. policy in Central America. One has been the fear of revolution, or instability, and the effect of such turbulence on how other world powers might judge our own stability and dynamism. The second of these fears is that we ourselves may actually become vulnerable to such turbulence, a fear that stems from our belief that other powers will try to infiltrate our hemisphere, seduce or overwhelm the nations of Central America and thus threaten our own security. These fears have allowed little if any room for us to consider the needs and desires of the Central American states themselves but result in policies that treat them (often brutally) as mere instruments in our own exercises of power. Thus we have intervened, politically and militarily, time and again in Central America, but have repeatedly failed to achieve a successful foreign policy in the region.

Our fear of vulnerability has another dimension, one that has made our efforts doubly ill-fated. In Central America the threats we have feared have never been actual—certainly not cause for U.S. intervention. In Central America we have fought, and are currently fighting, shadows. Today these are the shadows of Soviet-Cuban expansionism; in the 1920s they were the shadows of the avowedly leftist Mexican revolution; in the last century, the shadows of British imperialism. Yet we have preemptively and repeatedly intervened in the region. In this sense, we have never had a true "Central American policy" at all. In "dealing with Central America," the United States has been dealing with itself.

Our policies have, as a result, produced precisely those effects that we most feared. Today the American brand of democracy holds little ground in Central America, while allies and adversaries alike question the wisdom of our continued pursuit of failed policies. Rival ideologies (though not rival powers) seem to be gaining in strength—Leninism in Sandinista-ruled Nicaragua; Marxism among the Salvadoran rebels; rightist authoritarianism in Guatemala. Even Costa Rica, the only Central American state that has functioned for any significant period of time as a democracy, shows signs of internal strain. And in Honduras, a young and fragile democracy dominated by its armed forces, José Azcona Hoya, president of the ruling Liberal Party, has said that the U.S. military presence "will lead to the polarization and radicalization of Honduran society."[1] If so, then why are we there? Because, according to Azcona, "We are worrying about something that is not likely to happen," by which he meant the supposed threat from Nicaragua.

In addition to bringing about such undesired results, the policies of the United States with regard to Central America during the last hundred and sixty years have had another, perhaps even more serious effect: they have often prevented us from adequately appreciating the larger problems of the Latin Ameri-

6

can region as a whole. The Reagan Administration's current obsession with the affairs of the Central American states—and especially with three of them, El Salvador, Nicaragua and Honduras—has made Washington reluctant to address effectively broader and more important hemispheric issues—issues that not only are of great significance for the Latin American region and for U.S. foreign policy but also have increasingly important implications for the American domestic situation.

Chief among these larger concerns is the question of debt. Many Latin American nations, most notably Brazil, Argentina and Mexico, are faced with massive external debts to foreign commercial banks, foreign governments and international lending organizations. Recent estimates put the Brazilian debt at $93 billion, the Argentinian at $44 billion and the Mexican at $89 billion.[2] Much of the wealth of Latin American nations must go to paying off these debts. Short of actual default, most of those nations will almost certainly put ceilings on the amounts of their payments. Such developments could have profound effects on American banks (the largest of which would be hard hit, to the extent that we might even see sporadic instances of actual bank failures, though this is admittedly improbable), on the U.S. budget (the deficit of which, with a significant further loss in revenue, would rise even higher) and, as a result, on American citizens, who would likely be faced with higher interest rates and higher taxes.

But instead of focusing its efforts on solving the financial crisis, the Reagan Administration apparently believes that a military victory over Marxist-Leninist regimes and factions in Central America is the single most pressing issue in the Western Hemisphere, and it has concentrated U.S. monetary and diplomatic resources on this struggle. In fact, the poverty, grotesque inflation (running anywhere from 50 to 300 percent in the various Latin American nations) and political fragility that such debts produce are far greater causes of instability in the hemisphere than are the Sandinistas in Nicaragua or the FMLN (Farabundo Martí National Liberation Front) guerrillas in El Salvador; but the Reagan Administration either cannot or will not recognize this. Whatever the exact reasons for the Administration's failure to do so, the results for much of Latin America, including the five Central American states, have been the same: a consistent refusal by the United States to work toward a realistic solution of the region's most pressing economic problems, a general lack of internal stability (the very thing Washington professes to be striving for), and increased violence, both between factions and between states. In its determined pursuit of ideological phantoms, the Reagan Administration not only ignores but also contributes to the growth of a tidal wave of social and economic crises in the hemisphere.

Why is the United States apparently unable to recognize the true needs and desires of the Central (and, for that matter, Latin) American region? There are those historians who portray it as largely a matter of economics, of U.S. exploitation of the region. But while the economic development of Central America has certainly made it dependent on U.S. markets, and while U.S. interventions often reflected Washington's desire to protect U.S. businesses, U.S. policy would have been the same regardless of economic factors. Today, for example, the Reagan Administration's justification for U.S. intervention is the presumed threat to U.S. security. In view of the small U.S. economic stake in the region at the end of 1982—only 0.37 percent of direct U.S. investment abroad is in Central America—such a rationale does not seem disingenuous. Similar considerations have dominated the thinking of U.S. policymakers in the past, demonstrating clearly that the 160-year-old policy of the United States in Central America is based primarily on political and diplomatic considerations, the nature of which I shall examine in these pages.

Clearly it is time to abandon the policies that have resulted in our deepening military involvement in the region. To understand how such a shift might be accomplished, I first look at the whole sweep of U.S.–Central American relations, to see how our fears of instability and vulnerability have frustrated our efforts to bring democracy and stability to the five states of the region. I then report on the situation in Central America in the early 1980s to demonstrate how the policies of the Reagan Administration coincide with those of the past. And finally, I suggest new policies that might bring increased stability to Latin America as a whole, as well as an end to the conflict in Central America—for our present and long-established course can only perpetuate, and probably heighten, Central America's endless war.

2

Toward Central America the United States has always asserted the prerogatives of a great power. Originally this attitude grew out of the overwhelming American conviction that it was our destiny, our "Manifest Destiny," to control the entire North American continent; as time went by and Manifest Destiny became wishful, if not archaic, thinking, its assumptions were retained by the more permanent notion that if we were not actually to rule the continent, we were at least to have the single greatest influence over it. But always the idea has persisted that we must lead and the nations of Central America must follow. Thus, any attempt to examine the present involvement of the United States in the region must begin by looking at the years in which this attitude took hold.

In an age when the expression "American imperialism" has become, at the very least, an embarrassment, it is perhaps difficult for many of us today to fully appreciate that there was a time when the concept was not only accepted in this country, but a nearly divine directive. The belief that the United States had created the world's most enlightened form of government, and, moreover, that it was the destiny of its people both to expand their nation and to bring that enlightenment to new regions and new peoples, was not simply the bluster of ambitious newspaper editors or crusading ministers; it was the well-reasoned (if passionate) belief of the nation's greatest political thinkers and first leaders, the Founding Fathers. The success of the American Revolution was taken by them as confirmation of this idea, and the way seemed open for the actual process to begin. As President Thomas Jefferson wrote to James Monroe in 1801: "However our present interests may restrain us within our own limits, it is impossible not to look forward to distant times when our rapid multiplication will expand itself beyond those limits, and cover the whole northern, if not the southern continent, with a people speaking the same language, governed in similar form, and by similar laws."[3] In Louisiana and Florida, this process would involve actual annexation; in other areas, it would involve the creation of what Jefferson refers to as "similar" forms of government; in either case, the desired result was clear: the United States would be the enlightened and expanding leader of a continent-wide, and perhaps hemisphere-wide, group of nations, all of which would be modeling themselves on and aligning themselves with this country.

Such being the case, it is perhaps surprising that when Spain's Latin American colonies began their various wars of independence early in the nineteenth century, these efforts were greeted coolly by the United States, a response that had nothing to do with a concern for the Spanish empire itself, which was corrupt and ready for collapse. Nor did it stem from theoretical differences with the leaders of the Latin American movements, all of whom expressed republican beliefs and looked to their great northern neighbor, at least in the beginning, for inspiration and assistance. Why, then, did the United States show reluctance to support such Venezuelan revolutionaries as Bolívar and Miranda? The answer to this question is threefold, and crucial for any understanding of the present relationship of the United States not only to Central America but to South America as well.

First (and always a vast irritation to Latin American leaders), many of the Founding Fathers and their immediate successors did not believe that the Latin American peoples were capable of creating, on their own, the sort of "good government" (i.e., American-style democracy) that the Latin Americans themselves envisioned. The religious, social and political backgrounds of the Spanish colonies, these Americans believed, made this impossible. Jefferson himself wrote of the Latin American rebellions that "History . . . furnishes no example of a priest-ridden people maintaining a free civil government."[4] And in 1821 Secretary of State John Quincy Adams, the motivating force behind and eventual co-author of the Monroe Doctrine, stated: "I wished well to their cause; but I had seen and yet see no prospect that they would establish free or liberal institutions of government. . . . They have not the first elements of good or free government. Arbitrary power, military and ecclesiastical, was stamped upon their education, upon their habits, and upon all their institutions. Civil dissension was infused into all their seminal principles. War and mutual destruction was in every member of their organization, moral, political, and physical. I had little expectation of any beneficial result to this country from any future connection with them, political or commercial."[5]

Such an attitude was not, of course, universal. In 1820 Henry Clay rose in the House of Representatives to urge immediate recognition of the new Latin American states, and, speaking to Adams in particular but also to any who shared the Secretary of State's opinions, argued against what he thought to be a distinctly un-American attitude. "Will gentlemen contend," said Mr. Clay, "because those people are not like us in all particulars, they are therefore unfit for freedom?"[6] But Clay spoke in vain; it was Adams' opinions that determined the policy of the United States toward Latin America.

The second reason for the tepid reaction of the United States to the Latin American rebellions complemented the first and prefigured Manifest Destiny. It was, so Jefferson, and even Hamilton, believed, the ordained mission of the United States to spread its enlightenment over as much of the Western Hemisphere as possible; indigenous Latin American attempts at self-government, whether republican or otherwise, could only hinder such a pursuit. Washington supported the idea of a balance of power in Europe to help the United States protect its own institutions, and hence its own special mission. Indeed, Jefferson, far from desiring that the Spanish colonies should rebel against their king, thought it best that Spain maintain control of them "till our population can be sufficiently advanced to gain from it piece by peice [sic]."[7]

Adams, too, believed that any American support or

recognition of the Latin American states would hinder his own attempts, between 1818 and 1821, to buy Florida from Spain; he did not see the United States as having a "mission" to export democracy, yet he was an expansionist as regards North America, believing not only that the Latin Americans were incapable of creating good government (and thus any relations with their new rulers should be discouraged) but also that the United States was the only polity on the continent that could. He instructed his minister in London to inform the British government that Britain ought not to view with alarm every possibility of America's extension "to our natural dominion in North America." Most Spanish territory had already been purchased by the United States. And "this rendered it still more unavoidable that the remainder of the continent should be ours."[8] Thus, from the very onset of Latin American independence, the United States was hostile to instability and revolution in the region, not because of any serious evaluation of the needs and/or capabilities of the emerging states, but rather because of our own desire to expand—in the words of Adams' great contemporary John C. Calhoun, "the passion for aggrandizement was the law paramount of man in society."[9] And expansion was coupled with our need to demonstrate the vitality and power of our own form of democracy.

The third reason for our indifference to republican movements in Latin America concerned not ourselves, but the powers of Europe. For though we insisted on predominance in our own hemisphere and believed that we were the only nation that could bring it good government, this rationale alone would, in all likelihood, never have been sufficient grounds for the enunciation of the Monroe Doctrine. Had the United States been left to its own devices, it would probably have pursued its goals in the hemisphere quietly, without a pronouncement to the rest of the world. Indeed, we were, in 1821, trying to do just that. Thus the third reason for our lack of interest in internal Latin American affairs: no *other* power seemed particularly interested, either. That situation, however, would shortly change.

The 1820–1822 rebellion within Spain itself forced King Ferdinand VII to accept not only a constitution but also the prospect that he would have to view his troubled colonies in Central and South America as forever lost. The event shocked Europe. The Holy Alliance of Russia, Prussia and Austria was stunned and frightened by this new and outright challenge to its sovereignty, power and philosophy. England, only recently separated from the Alliance, feared that the Continental nations would use the Spanish situation as an excuse to assert their own power, not only in Europe but also in various contested parts of the Western Hemisphere: Latin America, California, Oregon, the northern Pacific and, of course, Mexico. Europe went into a kind of panic, and that panic was to have a profound effect on the United States.

At first it seemed that there might be little reason for President Monroe and his Secretary of State to worry. Though the pronouncements of the Holy Alliance were filled with imperial rhetoric, none of the Allies seemed, initially, ready to move from rhetoric to action: Austria was more concerned with the threat of republicanism in Spain than with the idea of reasserting Ferdinand's rule over his colonies; Russia's Alexander I might have been more willing to assist Spain in the New World but knew that he could do so only in concert with the French; but the French prime minister, Joseph de Villèle, was far more concerned with the internal affairs of his own nation than with events in the Spanish empire. Thus the United States had reason to believe that its slow but steady accumulation of both territory and influence in the Western Hemisphere could continue.

But in 1823 events in Europe took a different course, and officials in the United States assumed (and it is important to note that this was an assumption, not a careful assessment) that the implications for their own hemisphere would also change. France grew more bellicose, despite Villèle's reservations, and invaded Spain to rescue Ferdinand from the republicans who were holding him a virtual hostage. Russia supported the move wholeheartedly, as did Austria, and talk of the Holy Alliance taking steps to restore Ferdinand's empire to him became common. England, now isolated in Europe, grew ever more anxious about her world position. And that anxiety caused her foreign minister, George Canning, to turn to an unlikely source for assistance: the United States.

It is the conventional wisdom that the United States used the British navy to legitimate a policy that it could not have effectively implemented on its own.

This is, to a large extent, true. Britain feared a shift in the European balance of power; America feared the interference of the Holy Allies in her plans for the Western Hemisphere, or, at very least, the northern half of it. America had the moral justification for joint action, stating that it was the right of the Latin American colonies to determine their own future (although, as we have seen, Washington's own intention of allowing them to do so was itself questionable); the British had the *de facto* justification in their fleet; and the end result was the Monroe Doctrine, stating that no European powers were to interfere in the political affairs of the New World.

But there are important aspects to the formulation of the Monroe Doctrine which, though frequently ignored, are important to the history of U.S.–Central American relations. Chief among these is the question of the threat from the Holy Alliance. Careful examination of the European situation in 1823 reveals the following:

- French prime minister Villèle, though resigned to intervention in Spain, had no intention of intervening in the Americas as well, which he believed would have been both futile and disastrous for France's economy.
- The Russian czar, as a result, could not consider such action; Russia had neither the fleet nor the economic rationale for independent action.
- Austria, under Metternich, was concerned solely with suppressing republicanism in

Europe; events in the New World remained of
no great significance to her.
· The British knew all this.

The Monroe Administration was, in all likelihood,
also aware of this. As historian Ernest May has
pointed out, "It is probably fair to judge that the
American decision makers had adequate evidence for
a just assessment of the situation abroad. If they chose
to make unrealistic estimates of the possible conse-
quences of the options open before them, they were
rationalizing arguments for courses of action which
they preferred for other reasons."[10] May adds that one
such reason was probably the upcoming presidential
election. Many members of Monroe's Cabinet wanted
the presidency, and their statements about Europe
could gain or lose them votes. But while all this was
doubtless true, it was also—as far as Central America
and, at this point, all of Latin America was concerned
—irrelevant. What was relevant to those emerging
countries was Washington's decision to accept an ex-
aggerated appraisal of the Holy Alliance's threat to
Latin America (perhaps out of a genuine, if unrealistic, fear) as the basis for a proclamation which would
ensure its own hegemony over the region.

Not for the last time, the United States was acting
on the fear of a *supposed* threat. But was the action
wholly duplicitous, a way to gain absolute control of
the Western Hemisphere? Certainly, in 1823, fears of
Europe among both elected officials and average citizens in the United States were high, high enough to
cause a national panic if it were even suspected that

the European powers truly meant to assert themselves. It is quite possible that, in this instance, genuine (though ungrounded) fear and political opportunism worked hand in hand; it would certainly not be the last time such would occur. Whatever the case, the result for the new nations of Latin America was the same: the United States did not mean to leave the business of running the Western Hemisphere up to them.

Among those new Latin American nations was the United Provinces of Central America, a nation that incorporated the five Central American states and declared its independence on July 1, 1823. But the five states, then as now, were too competitive to act as a genuine union. They were highly factionalized, each faction centering around one of the major cities of the region and in general controlled by that small portion of the population which could claim genuine Spanish heritage rather than Indian, black (many slaves from both North America and the Caribbean region had emigrated to Central America) or, as was most often the case, mixed. This had been true when the five states were Spanish colonies (they were, as more than one historian has said, the "backwater" of the Spanish empire), and independence did little to change things. It is therefore not surprising that virtually the first event to occur in the history of the United Provinces was a civil war.

Out of this civil war a leader emerged: Francisco Morazán. A Honduran by birth, Morazán was committed to the idea of Central American union. Among his personal political priorities were to weaken the Church, encourage religious toleration and establish a progressive legal system; chief among his fears were the threat to the United Provinces from Mexico, and the continued strife caused by conservative factionalists and the Church. For all these reasons, it seemed natural that Morazán should seek the assistance and protection of the United States. And yet, throughout his struggle to make the United Provinces of Central America a secure reality, which ended with his execution at the hands of his enemies in 1842, Morazán received no such help. Thus, the opening years of the history of independent Central America were accompanied not only by the factionalism and violence that would mark the region's history for generations to come, but also by the failure of the United States to intervene on behalf of a man and a movement that had a chance (even if a small one) to improve social and political conditions in the Central American states.

It is not difficult, given American attitudes, to see why this was so. Morazán's success would not only have been an obstacle to U.S. goals in Central America; it also raised the issue of whether or not a united Central America would act as its own nation and, perhaps, seek the help and friendship of nations other than our own. That Morazán sought the assistance of the United States rather than any other power, that an indigenous Central American form of democracy might actually have helped to stabilize the general situation in the Western Hemisphere, were not considered by U.S. policymakers. Democracy, if it were to come to Central America, would come from the United States, which could then control not only its nature but its associations and its future status.

Some will say that American economic interests were the main reason for our failure to support Morazán, and to be sure, those interests were expanding during the time of the United Provinces. But such interests would have expanded regardless of whether Morazán had succeeded; indeed, he probably would have encouraged such expansion. Economic motivations alone do not explain our actions. Our failure to support the United Provinces was, at heart, a political decision, a decision based on both world and local political anxieties.

3

Following the death of Morazán and the failure of the United Provinces, Central America settled into the political configuration we know today. The five nations became independent entities, and within each, social and political patterns (they could hardly be called structures) began to crystallize. Two features were common to the five states: internal upheaval and fear of Mexico, which periodically displayed predatory ambitions. The first of these features was a result of the near-universal failure of popular elections in Central America. Then as now, they were neither the common nor the most effective method of changing governments in the region. As future Secretary of State Henry L. Stimson wrote of Nicaragua in 1927, "It remains literally true that no Nicaraguan election has ever produced a result which was contrary to the wishes of the man or party which was in control of the government. Under such conditions, the only way left to these people to dispossess from the government a man or a party which was in control of it was by force. . . . Revolution thus became and for nearly a century has constituted a regular part of their political system."[11]

As to the fear of Mexico, it was to rise to such a point that in 1849 the Nicaraguan minister in London asked the United States whether Honduras, El Salvador and his own country might be admitted to the Union; when nothing came of that, he asked that the United States at least defend their territorial integrity.

But the United States had what it considered far weightier matters to deal with than the territorial integrity of the nations of Central America. Foremost was its own expansion, which, under President James Polk, resulted in the Mexican War, by which means the United States gained New Mexico, Arizona and California. Second, and almost as urgent as far as many Americans were concerned, there was the question of what to do about British ambitions in North America.

In the late 1840s Great Britain was making suspicious moves throughout the continent, in Canada, Oregon, California, Mexico—and in Central America, where it held Belize (on the Guatemalan coast), the Bay Islands and the Miskito Coast of Nicaragua on the Atlantic. This last was particularly vital, as it included the port of Greytown, or San Juan del Norte, which would have been the eastern terminus of a Nicaraguan canal from the Atlantic to the Pacific (an idea that, at the time, was at least as popular as that of a canal through Panama). It was true that most British moves during this period were aimed at expansion of trade alone, but even the possibility of extended British influence on the continent was enough to alarm a United States that still had vivid memories of the War of 1812.

No one felt this antipathy more strongly than President Polk. Following the conclusion of Mexican-American hostilities, he attempted to organize the five states of Central America in an effort to expel the British from their holdings. But the factionalized five states could not be lured into such a venture. Polk's aggressive sentiments, however, did not go unnoticed in London. Though the British public had little interest (as it would throughout the nineteenth century) in a confrontation with the United States, there were those government officials, notably Lords Palmerston and Clarendon, who did not shrink from such a prospect. And when, in 1848, the British set up a puppet state known as "Mosquitia" on Nicaragua's Atlantic coast, it appeared to be an open rejoinder to Polk's attempts to expel them, a process that would take twelve years, and would, ultimately, secure for the United States preeminent power in Central America.

The 1848 situation was briefly defused by the signing of the Clayton-Bulwer Treaty in 1850, by which Britain and America agreed to be partners in any future Nicaraguan canal ventures. But the effect was short-lived. When Franklin Pierce entered the White House, he declared that he would "not be controlled by any timid forebodings of the evil of expansion."[12] Once again, the British were put on their guard. But their own involvement in the Crimean War later in the decade prevented any decisive showdown with the United States. Palmerston and Clarendon could do little more than watch developments as capitalists (among them Cornelius Vanderbilt) and filibusterers —private adventurers capable of amassing huge power and influence in the five states—gave the United States an ever tighter grip on Central America.

But Palmerston and Clarendon still expected some

kind of confrontation with the United States. It was Palmerston's opinion that "In dealing with Vulgar minded Bullies, and such unfortunately the people of the United States are, nothing is gained by submission to Insult and wrong."[13] While most British politicians and the British public did not want outright hostilities with the United States, they did feel that a show of weakness in the face of expanding U.S. power was undesirable. By the mid-1850s it seemed once more possible that Central America could be the scene of an active demonstration of Anglo-American rivalry.

The curious case of William Walker brought matters to a head. Walker, certainly the most flamboyant of the filibusterers, actually managed to install himself as ruler of Nicaragua for two years, and the United States government recognized him. It was, as far as Palmerston was concerned, an undisguised insult, worthy of reaction; but still, the British public, the Crimean situation having left them war weary, would not support the idea of direct intervention. If the British wanted a show of strength but were unwilling to act, there seemed only one course left: convince the Central American states themselves to do it. If they could be made to see that the continued growth of U.S. influence would mean a proportionate loss of their own sovereignty, they might react accordingly and blunt the Yankee advance.

But Palmerston and Clarendon were met with much the same reaction that Polk had faced: the Central American states were far too concerned with their own internal rivalries, social and political, to take effective, concerted action against any larger power, especially one that was coming to play an increasingly vital role in their various economies. This final demonstration of Central American futility was enough for Clarendon, who declared, in 1857, that "those wretched mongrels in Central America are absolutely inviting aggression. Their utter inability to do anything but cut each other's throats and the proofs they have recently afforded that neither common danger nor common interest can induce them to unite offer temptations to filibusters which cannot be resisted. . . . We may be sure that sooner or later those countries will be overrun and occupied just as have been Louisiana, Texas, and California added to the Union."[14]

Before long Palmerston, the last holdout for confronting the United States in Central America, would also come to this conclusion. In 1860 arrangements were made for Britain to surrender the Miskito Coast and the Bay Islands, though they would continue to exercise control over Belize. And in his Annual Message of that same year, President James Buchanan, another expansionist American leader, announced that he was fully satisfied with the new arrangement.

Thus ended the only period in which a U.S.-British conflict in Central America was even remotely possible. Yet for the next half-century, a period during which the single most massive expansion of American political and economic influence in Central America was to occur, the United States government would consistently give voice to the fear of British ambitions in the region. Were those fears justified? Insofar as they implied that the British intended to increase their trade advantages and their financial dealings in the five states, yes; but such increases were not crucial, nor did they threaten the security of the United States. But Anglophobia was a powerful sentiment in the United States in the nineteenth and early twentieth centuries, and its leaders found many good uses for it in the five Central American states.

Following the American Civil War, the economic process that would eventually lead to complete Central American dependency on the United States moved faster. The five states had succeeded in producing agricultural products for export and were becoming closely tied to the North American market. In Guatemala these products were coffee, bananas and cotton; in Honduras, the quintessential "banana republic," bananas and coffee; in El Salvador, coffee; in Nicaragua, coffee, sugar and cotton; and in Costa Rica, coffee, bananas and sugar. The land became greatly concentrated in the hands of a few owners; since the demand for workers was seasonal, these large landowners became very powerful, in effect an oligarchy dominating the government, while the peasants, or *campesinos,* were never able to save enough money to own their own land.

The result was increased fighting in the five states. By the 1880s the U.S. government was warning that such conflicts threatened business interests. Since this did not seem enough reason to pacify the feuding Central Americans, Washington added that such conflicts could, if aggravated, lead to British military intervention. The peoples of Central America once again ignored Washington's warnings, either because they did not believe them or because they did not care. Whatever the case, they had good reason to be skeptical. The suggestion that Britain, in the late nineteenth century, might be eager to quarrel with the United States over the issue of Central America can scarcely be justified. Indeed, in the boundary dispute between Britain and Venezuela in 1895, the British accepted a U.S. demand for arbitration, an occasion that allowed President Grover Cleveland's Secretary of State, Richard Olney, to announce, "Today the United States is practically sovereign on this continent, and its fiat is law upon the subjects to which it confines its interposition."[15]

In this period Britain's problems included women's suffrage, workers' rights and the Irish question at home; abroad, there was the growing challenge of the German empire and the Egyptian problem, and the first Boer War was in the making. It is highly unlikely that officials in the United States were ignorant of all this; and yet, as in the case of the Monroe Doctrine, they chose to act upon an inaccurate assessment of the facts. It is not hard to discover why.

Throughout the 1880s Secretary of State James G. Blaine was quietly going about the work of tying the Central American economies directly to that of the United States, a process that he referred to as "annexation of trade."[16] After the U.S. defeat of the Spanish empire in the Spanish-American War of 1898 and the ascension to the presidency of Theodore Roosevelt in 1901, this process was stepped up dramatically, resulting in the largest flow of U.S. capital into Central America in history. Whether the United States actually saw Britain as a threat to its moves into Central America or simply needed a devil to justify them would be immaterial were it not for the persistent tendency that Washington would continue to display, even to the present—the creation of an external threat to justify U.S. predominance in the region.

Those who argued that Britain was an actual threat often cited the danger to the new Panama Canal as justification for U.S. policy; yet the Panama Canal neither confirmed the actual existence of a British threat nor, in and of itself, altered the course of U.S.–Central American relations. As historian Walter LaFeber has aptly written, "The Panamanian passageway accelerated the growth of U.S. power in Central America. It also magnificently symbolized that power. But it did not create the power or the new relationship."[17]

The "new relationship" of which LaFeber speaks was announced by Theodore Roosevelt in 1904, when he stated that the United States intended to become the "policeman" of the Western Hemisphere. His statement was significant because it was aimed as much at internal unrest in the hemisphere as at external aggression. And internal unrest, in Central America especially, had grown to alarming proportions. Honduras alone, in the period 1892–1907, experienced seven separate revolutions. Neither Roosevelt nor his Secretary of State, Elihu Root, believed that the Central Americans themselves were capable of policing their own countries. Roosevelt declared that the various struggles for power in the five states "are nothing less than struggles between different crews of bandits for possession of the customs houses—and the loot."[18] If such were the case, and if U.S. trade and influence were to continue to grow, someone would have to try to keep order in the region. As of 1904, that someone was to be the United States. The classic U.S. fear of instability thus became national policy. It would remain so to the present day.

And where, during all this, were the British, whose persistent expansionist aims had provided both moral and political justification for our own increased control over the Central American states? We need look at only one example from this period to understand how much British influence in Central America had decreased, and how absurd had become the claim that that influence posed any threat to the security of the United States.

For that example we return to Nicaragua, the state that had provided Britain's one fleeting strategic holding in Central America. In 1909 the country was ruled, not surprisingly, by a dictator, José Santos Zelaya, who, though no more socially or politically progressive than his opponents or his counterparts in other states, did share one desire with the majority of his subjects: he wanted to reduce U.S. influence in Nicaragua. American leaders, both politicians and businessmen, were understandably hostile toward Zelaya, and made the most of the brutal aspects of his rule. In addition, they leveled a further charge against him—that he was pro-British.

In doing so, his American accusers ignored yet another fact: that the British star, far from burning bright, was hardly visible in Central America. In 1896, after all, Britain had backed down from a possible conflict with the U.S. over Venezuelan borders (though the issue would not be fully settled until 1899); in 1901 the Clayton-Bulwer Treaty had been nullified; in addition, British trade interests were being severely threatened, if not supplanted, by U.S. concerns, most notably Boston's United Fruit Company (known in Central America as "the Octopus"); even Belize, Britain's last stronghold in the region, had closer economic ties to New Orleans than to British home or colonial ports. On the international scene England had, by 1909, far greater worries about the European situation than the American—the likelihood of her causing trouble with the United States over Nicaragua was remote, if it existed at all.

And yet the United States would use the charge of Zelaya's supposed British connection, at least in part, to justify intervention in Nicaragua on behalf of the dictator's Conservative Party enemies, who staged a rebellion on, ironically, the Atlantic coast. The Conservatives had little hope of success without U.S. help. President Taft ordered the marines into the area, saying that Zelaya was destabilizing the region. The twin fears, instability and vulnerability, justified Washington's overthrow of a native Central American regime.

A man sympathetic to U.S. interests, Adolfo Díaz,

was placed in power. In a remarkably short time, Díaz went so far into debt to U.S. bankers that he had effectively sold most of Nicaragua to them. When a rebellion broke out against him in 1912, 2,600 U.S. troops were required to put it down. This time a U.S. garrison remained in Nicaragua after the hostilities had ended. Throughout these events, British forces and influence were nowhere to be seen. The Nicaraguan affair amounted to a clear demonstration that the British had little to say about events in the Central American states. The United States had finally assumed the position it had declared proper for it in the region; it would soon discover, however, that it was an achievement of dubious value.

As they would in generations to come, U.S. policymakers in the nineteenth and early twentieth centuries used the fear of another great power's possible intervention in the region to achieve their own goals in Central America. But again we must ask: Was that fear genuine? From 1845 to 1860 there was only a remote chance that the British might engage in a conflict, however small, with the United States; after that, the possibility disappeared altogether. But in the United States that fear persisted, and whether because of political opportunism or genuine insecurity (just as in the case of the Holy Alliance earlier), the result was that we completely disregarded Central America's own political goals and realities.

4

That the United States was an expansionist nation during the nineteenth century cannot be doubted. Most people throughout the series of crises and conflicts that provided our rationale for territorial expansion remained wholly behind the idea that it was right and just that U.S. power should spread as far as possible, and those who opposed the policy of annexation were never able, in any specific instance, to prevent it.

Nonetheless, such opposition did exist and is important to the history of American foreign policy, especially as it affected Central America. For although the opposition was never able to prevent any particular case of annexation, its cumulative effect was such that by the first decade of the twentieth century, not only were antiexpansionist (or, as they called themselves, "anti-imperialist") forces strong, but they would soon assume leadership of the nation —a trend that would have important implications for the five Central American states.

The 1846 Mexican War, when President James Polk was to obtain much of this nation's most valuable southwestern and western holdings, raised great controversy in its day, and this controversy was not confined to the arguments of Washington politicians.

There was first the question of whether Mexico had actually, as Polk maintained, been the aggressor, or if, in fact, General Zachary Taylor had provoked the conflict. Once the war was under way and it became clear that annexation in some degree was going to take place, the argument over who had started the war gave way to the issue of how much territory the United States was going to take from Mexico, and to whether those new holdings were to be slave or non-slave states. Both arguments were heated, and both contingencies, to those who opposed annexation and/or slavery, seemed fundamental denials of American principles. Antislavery and antiannexation journalists and intellectuals, such as Horace Greeley, Henry David Thoreau and Ralph Waldo Emerson, made impassioned pleas for the American people to remember the spirit in which their country had been born. In their opposition, they found themselves strangely allied with such proslavery politicians as John C. Calhoun, who, fearing that the new territories would be admitted to the Union with non-slave status (thus weakening the power of the proslavery bloc in Congress), opposed annexation.

None of these able and eloquent men could prevent the annexation of Mexican territory—but had it not been for such opposition, the United States might have expropriated far more of its southern neighbor's lands than it ultimately did. Indeed, the counterpart of the antiannexation movement at the time was the all-Mexico movement, whose name is ominously self-explanatory.

The next great example of expansion through

armed conflict with another nation, the Spanish-American War, at the turn of the century, was, as historian Frank Freidel has pointed out, far too brief to cause the kind of widespread opposition that the Mexican War had provoked. Despite this, opposition did exist, both in and outside Congress. The most persistent among these voices—and one of the few to acknowledge, at the time, that the Spanish-American War actually worsened conditions in several contested areas, notably Cuba—was that of Professor Charles Eliot Norton of Harvard. By participating in the war, said Norton, "we jettison all that was most precious of our national cargo."[19] Such statements were to earn him the reproach of colleagues and politicians alike, yet he persisted.

But what truly set in motion the series of events that would lead to the end of annexationism as a national policy was not the war with Spain, but one of its by-products, the Philippine insurrection. One of the terms of the treaty that concluded the war provided for Spain to sell the United States the Philippine Islands for the sum of $20 million. In the face of widespread Filipino resistance, President William McKinley realized that the United States not only would have to pay for the islands but would have to subdue them forcibly if annexation were to take place. It looked, even to many who had supported the war with Spain, suspiciously like conquest, and as the savagery of the American response to the insurrection (which ultimately cost as many as 200,000 Filipino lives) grew, opposition mounted.

The war dragged on for three long years, and during that time the United States was to learn, in graphic terms, the true cost of annexing a region whose inhabitants had no wish to be annexed. Newspaper reporters were dispatched to the islands and sent home tales of atrocities committed not only by the Filipinos but by American soldiers as well. Doubtless a fair number of these reports were yellow journalism, but in any case, sympathy with the Filipino rebels grew in the United States. In Chicago, the Anti-Imperialist League was formed, headed by such worthies as William Jennings Bryan; in Washington, Senator George Frisbie Hoar, an outspoken supporter of the Spanish-American War, gradually changed course and called for an end to the violence; while Charles Francis Adams, Jr., head of the Massachusetts Historical Society, and William James denounced the attempt to subdue an unwilling populace.

James was particularly eloquent: "There are worse things than financial troubles in a Nation's career. To puke up its ancient soul and the only things that give it eminence among nations, in five minutes without a wink of squeamishness, is worse; and that is what the Republicans would commit us to in the Philippines."[20] Even Mark Twain opened himself up to rebuke from expansionists when he said that in view of the Philippine insurrection, the American flag ought to have "the white stripes painted black and the stars replaced by the skull and crossbones."[21]

Once again, antiannexationists did not have the power to prevent a specific act of expansionism, and the Philippines were taken by the United States. But the overall tide was turning. Annexationism lost much of the feverish quality that had been notable throughout the nineteenth century. This was no doubt due in part to the settling of the continental boundaries of the United States, so that further annexation would necessarily involve overseas adventures similar to the Philippine fiasco. But the role of those opposed to annexationism as U.S. policy cannot be neglected. By 1900 Bryan, the avowed anti-imperialist, would gain enough popularity to run for President—and though he would not win, another man with similar principles would enter the same race just over a decade later, with Bryan's endorsement, and come away with a far different result.

Woodrow Wilson never left any doubt as to where he stood on the issue of expansionism. In October of 1913, the first year of his presidency, he declared, "I want to take this occasion to say that the United States will never again seek one additional foot of territory by conquest. She will devote herself to showing that she knows how to make honorable and fruitful use of the territory she has."[22] Wilson meant these words specifically to pacify the apprehensions of Latin American leaders and businessmen, who had, over the course of the previous few decades, grown understandably uneasy about the intentions of the United States. Wilson's attitude marks a turning point in the history of U.S.–Central American relations, for he was not only stating a policy that was, for him, a deep personal belief, he was also reflecting the changed attitude of the American public. Manifest Destiny, and the policy of annexationism that had accompanied it, were rapidly losing not only their practicality and their attraction—they were also losing their rationale. Two things were responsible for this: the rapid development of the United States Navy and the dramatic expansion of U.S. international trade.

The determined construction of a fleet that could rival those of the great European sea powers, England and Germany, together with the appearance of U.S. naval strategists such as Alfred Thayer Mahan, had given the United States, by the early twentieth century, the ability to influence events in distant and not so distant regions without actually annexing those regions. This power was generally sufficient to protect the lives and interests of those American capitalists whose concerns, in Central America as elsewhere, depended on stable native governments. Thus Wilson could state with both certainty and accuracy that trade had superseded annexation as the primary U.S. concern—for if the profits of trade could be had, and its agents protected, without the trouble of actual administration, then annexationism had indeed become an archaic concept. Such being the case, Wilson's comments on the nature of international trade ("I wonder if you realize, I wonder if your imaginations have been filled with the significance of the tides of commerce"[23]) were in fact the reflection of a very practical and momentous shift in the conduct of American foreign policy.

For no region did this shift hold greater significance than for Central America. Wilson's belief that the benefits of healthy trade would eventually cause more equitable, democratic governments to appear in the five states may have demonstrated his noble ambitions for the region—but it also displayed his almost complete ignorance of Central American history and politics. Moreover, his own background in English and American history and politics, as well as his moral fervor, compelled him to make his dealings with Central America conform to his own Anglo-American theories. Thus, he believed that revolution, when it meant seizing power by violating a constitution and the rights of individuals, was immoral.[24] But as we have already seen, such revolutions were, by Wilson's day, a well-established and integral part of the Central American political scene—and as Wilson would quickly learn, trade alone did little to change this. If anything, the profits brought by heavier trade only encouraged revolution, since so few of those profits found their way beyond the ruling oligarchies of the five states.

It was this dilemma that was to cause Wilson's chief problems in, and the ultimate frustration of his ambitions for, Central America. It would also lead him to become one of the leading exponents of the policy that was now to replace annexationism: interventionism. If annexation was finally out of the question in Central America (and by 1913, it was), and if trade failed to stabilize and in some cases *de*stabilized native governments there, then it was necessary to resort to a policy that would not bear the onus of the former but could protect the interests of the latter. Whether or not Wilson purposefully sought to develop such a third policy is doubtful; that he did, in the end, employ it

39

is unquestionable. The first outright demonstration of this occurred in 1914, in Nicaragua.

The man the United States had placed in power, Adolfo Díaz, though he had put down the rebellion of 1912 (with the help of U.S. troops), continued to find governing his people an arduous task. In 1914 he asked that the United States extend protectorate status to Nicaragua. In return, he was willing to give the United States full and exclusive rights over any future construction of a Nicaraguan canal. Wilson's Secretary of State, Bryan the anti-imperialist, urged acceptance of the deal, saying, "It will give us the right to do that which we might be called upon to do anyhow,"[25] i.e., ensure Nicaragua's internal stability in order to protect U.S. trade and financial interests, which, at this time, were impressive.

Wilson found himself in a bind. Although granting Nicaragua protectorate status would smack dangerously of expansionism, he felt very strongly that the United States had to check the growth of foreign, especially European, commercial dealings in Central America. For, much as Wilson believed in the evils of expansionism, he also harbored the traditional American distrust of foreign influence. "Who commonly seeks the intervention of the United States in Latin American countries?" he had asked. "Always the foreign interests, bondholders or concessionaries. They are the germs of revolution and the cause of instability."[26] Wilson was largely right, but he neglected to add that the American was among those "foreign interests" that accounted for instability. His belief in the purity of the American mission was supreme. In Walter LaFeber's words, Wilson "explicitly extended the Monroe Doctrine to European financial as well as political and military intervention."[27] Thus justified, Wilson felt that he could, in this case, compromise his beliefs about expansionism. He agreed to Nicaragua's request for protectorate status.

The United States Senate, however, did not. Demonstrating just how powerful antiannexationism had become in this country, the Senate refused to ratify the proposed treaty with Nicaragua until any and all mention of protectorate status was removed. This was eventually done, in 1916. But though the word was removed, the effect was the same. The Bryan-Chamorro Treaty not only ensured a *de facto* U.S. protectorate over Nicaragua (one that Wilson backed up with more marines), it also outraged other Central American governments that were alarmed about growing U.S. interests in the region, notably Costa Rica, which was, at this time, all but run by the United Fruit Company. Wilson, however, ignored all such objections, firm in his belief that it was the duty of the United States to exclude destabilizing foreign influences and bring its own form of enlightenment, through trade, to the region—even if the region could not effectively incorporate such gifts. As it would in so many other cases, Wilson's insistence on an ideal led him into very murky waters.

Further evidence of this attitude came in 1917, in the country that had become the leading critic of U.S. policy in Central America: Costa Rica. In that year a revolution brought General Federico Tinoco to power, a man who was offensive to Wilson for a variety of reasons, not the least of which was that he had used force to gain Costa Rica's presidency and was thus, in Wilson's view, an illegitimate ruler (though Wilson ignored similar behavior on the part of most other Central American leaders, including Díaz in Nicaragua, who had also assumed power through force). But Tinoco had other qualities that made him unacceptable to Wilson—he was closely associated with Minor Keith, the head of United Fruit and a man whom Wilson mistrusted; and he was also making overtures to British oil companies about possibly drilling in Costa Rican fields. As far as Wilson was concerned, such drilling would be done only by U.S. companies. Thus, he refused to recognize the legitimacy of Tinoco's government, and Tinoco was eventually forced out of power. Such hypocrisy, given the posi-tion of the United States in Nicaragua, did not affect Wilson's behavior; that it was the right of a Costa Rican leader (who was certainly as "legitimate" as most of his counterparts in the region) to determine who should drill for oil in his country's fields also did not affect the President's judgment. Two things alone were important, the same two things—though now in different guises—that had always been of central con-cern to the United States in Central America: the exclusion of foreign influence and the maintenance of stability in order to protect U.S. interests. If the philo-sophically expansionist rhetoric of Thomas Jefferson was gone, it had been replaced by the commercial rhetoric of Woodrow Wilson, declaring that trade was the method by which the civilizing influence of the United States was now to be exported. And when events threatened this policy, Wilson did not hesitate to intervene to shore it up—by the time he left office in 1921, Wilson had placed U.S. marines not only in Nicaragua but in Haiti and Santo Domingo as well. Committed to avoid annexation, he had endorsed a policy that, if not new, was certainly strengthened by his acceptance of it: interventionism. In the years to come, that behavior was to become habitual.

Washington's policy of intervention to ensure internal stability and exclude outside influences was to have its longest and clearest demonstration in Nicaragua, from 1924 to 1936. In 1924 U.S. marines were still in Managua, but the U.S. government was determined to get them out. An overly abrupt withdrawal, however, ran the risk of abandoning the country to chaos, and the White House therefore decided to wait until after the 1924 Nicaraguan elections. The elections were held, and a coalition ticket emerged victorious: Carlos Solórzano, a Conservative, became president, and Dr. Juan Sacasa, a Liberal, became vice president (it should be noted that the labels "Liberal" and "Conservative" had, as far as Central America is concerned, little ideological value; they reflected far more about a man's social and regional connections than about his personal beliefs). Immediately after the elections, Calvin Coolidge ordered the U.S. marines home.

Within weeks, the coalition government in Managua had fallen. The loser of the elections staged a coup, and both Solórzano and Sacasa were forced into exile, the latter to Mexico. The message was clear to Washington: Nicaragua was not yet ready for American-style democracy, unless American troops were present to supervise it. Coolidge sent the marines back in, accompanied by a special presidential adviser, Henry Stimson, with orders to settle the situation in Managua and redouble efforts to ensure that a functioning democracy would be created.

Stimson's first move was to place in power the old U.S. surrogate Adolfo Díaz, who could be relied upon to ensure future elections. Next came the question of the deposed coalition government. While Solórzano and Sacasa might have been viewed by many as the legitimate governors of Nicaragua, Sacasa's efforts to gain help from the revolutionary government of Mexico had effectively ruled out the possibility that Washington would allow the coalition to return to power.

It was a curious period in U.S.–Central American relations, one with evident parallels to the situation we face today. Ever since the long series of upheavals in what would become known as "revolutionary Mexico" had commenced in 1910, the United States had had great difficulty in coming to terms with that nation; relations had, under Wilson, deteriorated so badly that a U.S. expeditionary force had actually invaded Mexico. By the 1920s Mexican politicians were making bold pronouncements with decidedly socialist overtones, and there were officials in the United States who chose to interpret these statements as a reflection of Soviet Bolshevism. When Sacasa applied to these same Mexicans for assistance, Washington was put on guard. Mexico was doubtless trying to spread its own brand of socialism—whether or not Soviet-inspired, but certainly inimical to the interests of the United States—into Central America.

This attitude was officially expressed by Under Secretary of State Robert Olds in January of 1927: "The Central American area down to and including the isthmus of Panama constitutes a legitimate sphere of influence for the United States, if we are to have due regard for our own safety and protection. . . . We do control the destinies of Central America and we do so for the simple reason that the national interest absolutely dictates such a course. There is no room for outside influence other than ours in the region. . . . The action of Mexico in the Nicaragua crisis is a direct challenge to the United States."[28]

Such an attitude reflected an unwillingness to recognize two things: first, the nature of the Mexican revolution itself, and second, the nature of the Nicaraguan movement headed by Sacasa. As to the first of these, the socialist rhetoric employed by Mexican leaders was largely that, rhetoric, used by those in power to maintain the allegiance of an oppressed population. More important, there was no genuine threat to the United States of any sort of "internationalism" from Mexico—but again, the United States was ready to act on a *supposed* threat. As to the nature of Sacasa's Nicaraguan movement, it was, if anything, more conservative than the government of Mexico. Sacasa and his military co-leader, General José María Moncada, were revolutionaries only insofar as they were using the rhetoric of revolution to regain power.

But such thoughts were far from the minds of U.S.

policymakers. They viewed the Sacasa faction that had invaded eastern Nicaragua with Mexican help as a serious threat—ideologically as well as militarily and politically—and pressed for its defeat.

In this light, the actions of President Coolidge's special envoy, Stimson, become far more interesting. Stimson, a lawyer and diplomat, was apparently the one American who could accurately identify the Sacasa movement as merely another Central American faction pursuing national power. To this end, he urged Díaz to negotiate—not with Sacasa but with Moncada. Díaz would thus be exploiting rival ambitions to split the opposition. Stimson's suspicions proved true—Moncada, far from supporting the claims of his own leader, was more than happy to put himself forward as the co-signatory of a nationwide truce, knowing that it would, in all probability, lead to his nomination for president in the elections that Stimson was organizing for 1928. Pursuant to this, Moncada laid down his arms, as did his generals, with the exception of one: Augusto Sandino.

As 1928 and the new elections approached, the chief U.S. concern was how to keep order in Nicaragua without using the marines. The idea grew of creating a native Nicaraguan force, trained and initially commanded by members of the U.S. Army. This force, eventually to be known as the National Guard, was to remain outside politics and to concern itself only with maintaining order and ensuring fair elections. Nothing could have demonstrated more clearly the continued U.S. misunderstanding of the nature of Central American politics. Walter LaFeber points out that

"Only later—too late—did these officials understand that in Central America such a force would not remain above politics, but single-handedly determine them."[29] But Stimson and other Americans were convinced of the promise of the idea, and the Guard's strength was increased as each year went by.

Meanwhile, in the mountains of the north, the defiant Sandino was waging guerrilla war against what he termed the Yankee "occupation" of Nicaragua. Like his counterpart of fifty years later, Edén Pastora, Sandino declared that the Nicaraguan "revolution" had been betrayed, and that Moncada and those who followed him were traitors. Not surprisingly, when Moncada won the election of 1928, Sandino still refused to surrender, saying that he would not end the guerrilla campaign until the U.S. marines had left his country. In 1929 Herbert Hoover was inaugurated in the United States, and Henry Stimson became Secretary of State. They began a phased withdrawal of the marines, gradually turning over administrative control to the National Guard.

The case of Sandino is an interesting one, and not without its own parallels to the present Central American situation. Sandino himself, through his resistance to the American-backed Moncada administration, was widely romanticized as a heroic freedom fighter—but as in the case of many Central American leftist groups today, the facts did not and do not entirely warrant this label. In reality, Sandino maintained his control over the northern mountains as much through terror and extortion as through popularity. Though a personally charismatic figure, he was also capable of barbaric cruelty (demonstrated by his ritual machete executions of civilians who did not support him) and flights of arcane spiritualism. He was also undeniably ambitious. He never formulated a political philosophy based on anything more than the cult of personality or aimed at anything higher than the expulsion of foreign interests and U.S. marines—yet it was those same marines who had ensured the success of the 1928 election, which, even pro-Sandino historians will admit, was probably the fairest the country had ever known. The idealization of Sandino persists—understandably—to this day, perpetuated and propagated by the Sandinista rulers of Nicaragua, who attribute to his name beliefs and achievements, some of which it would be hard to prove he ever held or accomplished.

Despite Moncada's attempts to gain a second term for himself (something forbidden by the Nicaraguan constitution), Secretary Stimson made a particular point of seeing to it that the next elections would be at least as fair as in 1928, and therefore that Moncada would be frustrated. He succeeded on both counts. The 1932 elections were even more open than the ones in 1928, as the results show: Juan Sacasa was elected president. If the United States had decided to control the elections, as Sandino charged, President Hoover and Secretary Stimson could doubtless have found a more suitable candidate. But Hoover and Stimson were mainly interested in withdrawing the marines, and they could do this only after an election that was popularly viewed as fair. Once Sacasa had been inaugurated, the marines did leave.

With U.S. troops gone and his ex-leader in power, the time seemed right for Sandino to fulfill his pledge and lay down his arms. He did not. The National Guard became his new target, and he declared that he would not give up his fight until it was disbanded. The power of the Guard had grown dramatically, however, and Sacasa could hardly order its termination. Only when the war-weary peasants of the north refused, even under threat of retaliation, to perpetuate Sandino's struggle did he give up, saying, in 1933, "Now, when foreign intervention in Nicaragua has ceased, albeit in appearance alone, the people's spirits have cooled down. Political and economic intervention is suffered by the people, but they cannot see it —even worse, they do not believe in its existence."[30] It was a line of reasoning suspiciously close to that employed by his opponents. But lack of support in the mountains forced him to negotiate with Sacasa, whom he warned (accurately, if needlessly) of the rising power of the National Guard and its commander, Anastasio Somoza.

Somoza was typical of the leadership emerging in the 1930s in Central America. Educated, shrewd and more than willing to employ brutality, he had made his way up from poverty into the highest circles of Nicaraguan society and politics. That his goal was to be president few denied—but the extent to which he was to realize and consolidate this position was something equally few could have guessed.

In 1934 Somoza arranged the murder of Sandino. Two years later he was at least partially responsible for the creation of a national crisis, during which he became president. After that, he reorganized the political system (badly abusing the constitution) so that his own power would be perpetuated until his death and could thereafter be transmitted to his sons. The United States made no moves to prevent this. Weary and frustrated by the long involvement in Nicaragua, and now faced with global and domestic problems of far greater importance, Washington had shifted its policy in Central America. No longer would the United States try to encourage local democratic government to ensure stability—the Nicaraguan experience had led U.S. policymakers back to the conclusions of Jefferson and Adams: Central Americans were incapable of running an effective democracy on their own. But the goals of internal stability to protect U.S. interests and the exclusion of foreign influences were, if anything, of heightened importance in 1936. The simplest policy, given these considerations, was therefore to back that person (or party) in each Central American state who had the best chance of maintaining order and remaining loyal to the United States. In the case of Nicaragua, that man was Somoza. But he had his counterparts in Guatemala, in El Salvador and in Honduras—all of varying benevolence as rulers, but all firmly committed to stability and the United States.

Because of this new, highly expedient approach to the region, the United States failed either to adequately recognize or to support the only regimes that had been making any progress along democratic lines, those in Costa Rica. During the 1920s and 1930s, two men, Ricardo Jiménez Oreamuno and Cleto Gonzales

Víquez, alternated terms as president, and while they were certainly no more disposed to reducing their personal powers than were their counterparts in the other four states, the ends toward which these two men used those powers were far different. Recognizing the demands of their people for more equitable social conditions, they would, between 1924 and 1936, not only institute land reforms and increase political freedom (including the legalization of the Communist Party)—they would also pursue government programs that would eventually make it possible for Costa Rica to have the only working democracy in Central America.

All this was of little interest to the United States. With the memory of twenty-five years of frustration in Nicaragua fresh in their minds, U.S. officials entrusted Central America to a new and rising class: those who belonged to or controlled the military elites. These elites gained power during the Depression of the 1930s, and as their power grew, so did Washington's conviction that it had finally found a solution to the never-ending problem of Central America. Not that officials in Washington were ever deluded as to the nature of Central America's new brand of leader—as Franklin Roosevelt said of Somoza, "He's a son of a bitch, but he's ours."[31]

5

During World War II, U.S. and Latin American military officers cooperated closely to prevent any intrusion into the hemisphere by German or Japanese forces. By 1940 the United States had become the preeminent supplier of military equipment and instruction for Latin American armies, whose efforts (coinciding with Washington's own preferences) were centered as much on maintaining internal stability as they were on repelling any Axis aggression. The United States, especially during the early stages of global conflict, badly needed stability and support in its own hemisphere. In helping Washington pursue this goal, the leaders of Central America never wavered.

But by the end of the war the U.S. government had come to believe that the danger threatening Central America was no longer the Axis, nor was it Mexico or Britain—it was, in the words of Assistant Secretary of State for Inter-American Affairs Edward Miller, "Communist political aggression against the hemisphere."[32] The fear of Communism as the key determinant of U.S. policy toward Central America marks a serious turning point. For more than a century Washington had tried to deal with its two main Central American anxieties—instability and possible external threats—by saying that the encouragement of U.S.-

style democracy within the five states (whether through trade or intervention) was at least as high a priority as were the security guarantees it demanded. But with the arrival of the Cold War, such a rationale became distinctly less important. Much less was also heard about the need for markets, though the North American companies were still important and their interests in Central America were close to those of the State Department. The primary objective of U.S. policy was simply to keep the five states of Central America from going Communist. In struggling over three and a half decades to ensure this result, American Presidents and their advisers followed courses of action that would finally merge their fears of instability and vulnerability. This process would be fully realized in the Administration of Ronald Reagan—which would epitomize Washington's traditional unwillingness to recognize the realities of the Central American political scene.

In 1950 the U.S. State Department sent its ranking Soviet expert, George F. Kennan, to Rio de Janeiro to meet with U.S. ambassadors in South America. His interpretation of how Latin America fit into U.S. policy is still considered revealed truth by most policymakers, more than thirty years later. Kennan defined several goals: ensuring the safety of the region's raw materials (and their availability to the United States), seeing to it that Latin America could not be militarily exploited by the enemies of the United States (especially the Soviets), and preventing any outside ideological influence from turning the southern part of the hemisphere against us.[33]

Most important of all, as Kennan saw it, no Communists must be allowed in power. "It is better," he declared, "to have a strong regime in power than a liberal government if it is indulgent and relaxed and penetrated by Communists."[34] Secretary of State John Foster Dulles, perhaps alarmed over the new reformist government in Guatemala, expressed similar sentiments when he warned, a few years later: "Conditions in Latin America are somewhat comparable to conditions as they were in China in the mid-thirties when the Communist movement was getting started. . . . If we don't look out, we will wake up some morning and read in the newspapers that there happened in South America the same kind of thing that happened in China in 1949."[35]

Nothing of the kind was going to happen under Dulles. In 1954, in a celebrated triumph of covert action, the Central Intelligence Agency masterminded a coup that overturned the government of Jacobo Arbenz Guzmán, who had legalized the Guatemalan Communist Party. He had also instituted land reform and threatened to expropriate the holdings of the United Fruit Company. When he began importing weapons from the Soviet bloc, he was done for.

Initially, Dulles tried to get other Latin American nations to intervene in Guatemala because, he argued, Communist political power (and there were Communists in the Arbenz government) was "more dangerous than open physical aggression."[36] When almost no support was forthcoming from the surrounding countries (in keeping with historical tradition), the stage was set for covert action to bring down Arbenz. The coup went off smoothly, largely because the army was angry that Arbenz had equipped a militia composed of workers and peasants. As the American ambassador on the scene proudly reported it, the coup had been only "forty-five minutes off schedule."[37]

The "success" of the coup, however, did not bring democracy to Guatemala—as we have seen, the achievement of democracy was no longer the primary or even the secondary concern of the U.S. government. In their valuable study *Bitter Fruit,* Stephen Schlesinger and Stephen Kinzer recount the attempts of Washington's agent of counterrevolution, Colonel Carlos Castillo Armas, to rule by bribery and decree until he was finally assassinated, in 1957, by a disaffected soldier. Castillo's military clique maintained itself in power until, after a series of elections, General Miguel Ydígoras Fuentes, a rightist and an exiled military leader, finally was elected in 1957 for six years. His policy, in turn, gave rise to guerrilla activity on the part of idealistic young officers; but with American help, their revolt was crushed in 1962.

A year later another coup took place and yet another Guatemalan dictatorship was installed. This time Washington may not have been directly involved but knew what was happening and at least tacitly encouraged it. The sorry story of Guatemala to this day is one of increasing military control of the entire society. As Schlesinger and Kinzer put it: "The intention of the military leaders was essentially to destroy the political center. Anyone not supporting the regime was almost by definition a leftist, and therefore an enemy. The military apparently believed that eliminating the center precluded the possibility of a moderate government, therefore leaving the country a sterile choice between a revolutionary Communist regime and the existing military dictatorship."[38]

In 1961 President John F. Kennedy established the reformist Alliance for Progress to forestall violent revolution, but this did little to put any distance between the United States and the military in Central America. Luis and Anastasio Somoza ruled comfortably in Nicaragua (their father having been assassinated in 1956), while the armed forces consolidated their power in Guatemala. In Honduras and El Salvador, however, democratic forces were gaining strength—and Costa Rica, with no army since 1948, was creating a democracy. Kennedy apparently hoped that if democratic forces could be built up in some parts of Latin America, this would encourage the growth of democracy elsewhere in the region.

Unfortunately, the Alliance for Progress got off to a less than convincing start: a month after Kennedy announced that the United States would send $100 billion to Latin America during the next decade, Cuban exiles trained by the CIA suffered the humiliating disaster of the Bay of Pigs. Moreover, Kennedy's rhetoric of revolutionary change awakened hopes that were never fulfilled. It was not long before Kennedy himself admittedly felt "depressed" (a word that Theodore Sorensen refers to as "rare in his vocabulary") about "the size of the problems that we face

. . . the population increases, the drop in commodity prices . . . serious domestic problems. . . . The Alliance for Progress . . . has failed to some degree because the problems are almost insuperable, and for years the United States ignored them and . . . so did some of the groups in Latin America. . . . In some ways the road seems longer than it was when the journey started."[39]

The Alliance for Progress had from the start concentrated as much on combating violent revolution as on granting economic aid for development. In Latin America, this meant training the police and military for counterinsurgency campaigns. In Central America, in 1963, Washington helped to establish the Central America Defense Council, or CONDECA, for the region's collective security. (Costa Rica remained outside it and repeatedly condemned it.) By now the pattern was set for relying on the military to keep order and even to be the agent of social change.

Under Lyndon Johnson, the security aspect of the Alliance came to dominate policy; Johnson himself referred to Kennedy's habit of making impassioned calls for "revolutionary" changes in the social structures of the Latin American states while at the same time dealing with the military elites to ensure both internal, non-Communist stability and the preferred status of U.S. business interests, as "a lot of crap."[40] The Johnson Administration effectively shook off any remnants of Kennedy's commitment to counteract Castroism by offering economic aid designed to stimulate social reform. Military support, however, suffered no such fate. Washington may have had hopes for a professional and politically neutral military that would be more open to democracy, but it never posed firm conditions on the ruling groups it dealt with to stop military repression.

LBJ's policies, based on the notion that constructive social change could come about almost solely through the actions of the military, remained largely in place during the Nixon years. In his report prepared for Congress in 1969, Nelson Rockefeller, whom Nixon had sent to Latin America to come up with a new policy, recommended a military solution to unrest in the region. He pointed out that since 1961, when Kennedy's Alliance for Progress had begun, "There have been seventeen coups d'état in the other American republics, much more than in any comparable period in the history of the Western hemisphere." Most of these had been caused by military factions, and Rockefeller might have denounced such behavior. But he went in the other direction. "Without some framework for order, no progress can be achieved." It followed that an American policy to provide training and equipment for the police and military "will bring about the best long-term hope for . . . improvement in the quality of life for the people." Although Rockefeller made some economic recommendations, he concluded that "the essential force of constructive social change" was the military.[41]

Meanwhile, foreign economic aid was being further reduced, in part as a response to the growing U.S. balance-of-payments deficits; but military aid continued, and loans to allow Central American armed forces to buy more arms were plentiful. Between 1973 and 1980, the annual cost for Central America's oil imports rose from $189 million to $1.5 billion.[42] With huge military establishments to pay for, there was little extra to go around. The region was ripe for revolution—and revolution came.

Jimmy Carter wanted to shift Latin American policy from Nixon's emphasis on power politics. He entered office stressing his commitment to human rights. In its contradictions and other failings, his policy turned out to be the moral equivalent of Kennedy's Alliance for Progress. In some South American countries, such as Brazil and Argentina, his pressure for human rights no doubt saved lives and freed political prisoners. Though more quixotic than Kennedy, Carter also wanted change without revolution in Central America, but he did not even pretend to offer economic incentives to prevent revolutionary situations from erupting.

The 1979 Nicaraguan revolution that finally brought down the Somozas cruelly heightened Carter's dilemma. It was clear by the late 1970s that Anastasio Somoza (Luis having died in 1967) and his hated National Guard were losing control of the country. Their greed had gone too far, along with the torture and repression, culminating in the assassination of Pedro Joaquín Chamorro, the respected publisher of *La Prensa*. Most of the social and political groups in Nicaragua, including the leading businessmen and clergy, joined in opposing Somoza. The Carter Administration was not unsympathetic to seeing the end of the Somoza dynasty, but feared a takeover by the left. The Soviet invasion of Afghanistan served further to strengthen the position of the hard-line anti-Communist forces in the Administration.

Characteristically, Carter waffled. Hoping to miti-gate the dictator's excesses and to avoid a second Cuba in Central America, Carter sent a secret letter to Somoza congratulating him on improving his re-cord on human rights and urging him to widen the political system. His entreaty was foolish and useless; within a few weeks Somoza embarked on a new round of massacres. Too late, the Administration sought a middle ground where there was none. Carter tried to keep the National Guard in business until the Nica-raguan elections, which were scheduled for 1981. He wanted to avoid dealing with a takeover by the San-dinista front, which was dominated by Marxists, though it also included non-Marxist business and pro-fessional men. Carter clearly had no use for Somoza, but "order" had to be maintained even if Somoza had to go. The Carter Administration called for a peace-keeping force made up of members of the Organiza-tion of American States, but got nowhere. Finally the Sandinistas took over. They publicly promised to maintain political pluralism, a mixed economy and a foreign policy of nonalignment.

Once again, Carter reversed his course. With the triumph of the revolution, Washington sent in nearly $20 million in aid. A few months later, in September 1979, Carter asked Congress to appropriate $75 mil-lion more in aid for Nicaragua. But by this time Carter had lost all effective control over Congress— which had never been strong at best. Congress did not even debate the request until January 1980, and finally passed the aid measure six months later. By this time Nicaragua, near bankruptcy, had concluded a series of trade agreements with the Soviet bloc. The Sandinistas had already postponed elections, and by the end of the year they had prohibited opposition political rallies and tightened censorship.

Whether Carter and Congress, by giving too little too late, missed an opportunity to influence the Sandinistas to follow a more democratic path is questionable. But it is undeniable that the Carter Administration's actions reflected the traditional American objectives—maintaining internal order in Nicaragua and blocking Soviet/Cuban influence.

Further evidence of this was offered in El Salvador, where there was also, during the early 1970s, something like a democratic tendency. In 1972 Christian Democrat José Napoleón Duarte won the presidency and Guillermo Ungo (now a member of the FMLN front) was named vice president. But the military overturned the elected government, and the middle all but disappeared. Both Duarte and Ungo went into exile. Revolutionary bands grew stronger, and terror from the extreme right became endemic. Finally, in 1979, a group of junior officers overthrew the corrupt military regime and announced a program of moderate reform, including some redistribution of wealth. It was also committed to eliminating the guerrilla movements.

The problem for the reform-minded officers was how to bring about land redistribution without destroying the army as an institution, since so many older officers were clearly tied in with the small group of rich landowners that depended on the army for support. The new government included several prominent moderate politicians, among them Guillermo Ungo; but cabinet members with close ties to the oligarchy were able to block all attempts at reform. (The police killed 160 people during the junta's first week in power.) In December the cabinet issued an ultimatum to the armed forces to submit to the authority of the civilian government. When this was ignored, the cabinet resigned, in January 1980. Unable to influence the right-wing military establishment, five of the leading military reformers fled the country later that year. A conservative military junta took over.

Once again, Washington relied on the military officers, many of whom had been trained in the United States. The Carter Administration asked Congress for $5.7 million in military supplies to "help strengthen the army's key role in reforms." As usual, the land reform program never got very far, and the Salvadoran army officers in charge showed little disposition to allow democratic political activity to take place.[43]

By the end of the Carter years, the various guerrilla movements had followed Havana's advice and organized themselves into a broad coalition; the new revolutionary front now included moderates such as Ungo, and even some Christian Democrats. Was there any chance that the groups associated with the guerrillas could be split apart so that the more moderate among them would work with what remained of the Christian Democrats? This was not Carter's approach. The danger, as Washington now saw it, was a victory for the revolutionaries.

To forestall that possibility, Carter ended his term by recommending that sizable military aid be given to the Salvadoran junta, a policy which the incoming Reagan Administration would both understand and follow. It was the last of many self-contradictory moves by the Carter Administration in Central America, and it prefigured both the policies of the Reagan Administration and the conclusions that would later be reached by Reagan's Bipartisan Commission on Central America. As Walter LaFeber puts it, "Carter wanted it both ways: decrease governmental coercion and publicly attack (and hence de-legitimate) the military regimes, while at the same time urging those regimes to fight the revolutions."[44]

In pursuit of this unattainable goal, Carter attempted both to maintain Somoza's rule over Nicaragua and to control the abuses of the National Guard, the very instrument of Somoza's power. He decried the murders of North American nuns and moderate Salvadoran political leaders in El Salvador, yet recommended substantial military assistance for the very junta that controlled those who were, in all probability, responsible for the murders. While such policies lacked the recklessness of Reagan's, they did, through their confused morality and even more contradictory policy priorities, contribute almost as greatly to the deterioration of the political situation in Central America.

During the thirty-five years following the end of World War II, no effective progress was made in dealing with the continuing problem of internal unrest in Central America—in several respects, ground was actually lost. Each year that the United States renewed its reliance on military elites and authoritarian rulers, the agents of social change in the region were forced to seek help elsewhere, most notably in Cuba, and its ally and protector, the Soviet Union.

Far from recognizing and removing the twin fears of instability and vulnerability, then, the United States, from 1945 to 1980, only gave them greater scope. The contradictory policies of the Carter Administration echoed the original policy failures of early-nineteenth-century American leaders—democracy (or at least a more equitable social and political structure) was desirable in Central America, but the states themselves could not be trusted to create this. Jimmy Carter's belief that the military could be the agent of social change recalled the views of Lyndon Johnson and Richard Nixon, and equally betrayed the true reasons for U.S. reliance on the elites: the need for internal stability and the exclusion of foreign influences.

The consistency of the United States' 160-year-old policy toward Central America is remarkable. And with the election in 1980 of Ronald Reagan, Washington's fears of revolution and of external threats to the region—and its willingness, even determination, to use force to combat them—were stronger than at any other time in America's history.

PART
11

1

The Reagan Administration has viewed turmoil in Central America almost exclusively through the lens of the Cold War. Reagan ran on a Republican platform that deplored "the Marxist attempts to destabilize El Salvador, Guatemala, and Honduras." Trouble in the region, the President declared three years later, could be ascribed to "revolution exported from the Soviet Union and from Cuba." As he has pointed out time and again, "If you go to the source" of the trouble in the region (he might have said the world), "I think you're talking about the Soviet Union."[1] The Defense Department shares this view. Deputy Assistant Secretary of Defense Nestor D. Sanchez has declared that "the Soviet Union is abetting an assault on this hemisphere more dangerous than the postwar threat to Western Europe."[2]

The broad lines of U.S. policy toward Central America remain what they have been since the enunciation of the Monroe Doctrine: to eliminate external "threats" to the countries of the region, and to maintain internal stability. While we have been carrying out this policy, the views of the Central American states themselves, as well as those of the regional powers, have largely been disregarded. Instead, the Reagan Administration has pursued a policy of increased militarization in the region, the hardly surprising result of which has been a dramatic heightening of violence and of general social and political tensions as well. In the face of this, negotiations—between the various competing factions within each state, between the states themselves, and between the states and Washington—have become an increasingly difficult and unlikely prospect.

Ronald Reagan inherited contrasting political situations in Nicaragua and El Salvador. In Nicaragua, the Sandinistas were reneging on their earlier promises: to pursue a foreign policy of nonalignment, preserve a mixed economy and ensure political pluralism. In fact, the Sandinistas had drawn closer to Cuba, importing some 6,000 Cuban advisers. Many of them worked in health and education but were also to have a growing influence in the grass-roots organizations and in training the new Nicaraguan army, which soon, with 50,000 troops, became the largest in Central America. And Cubans were helping to organize Nicaragua's intelligence and internal-security apparatus.

The Sandinistas were also aligning their foreign policy closer to that of the Soviet Union: for example, they refused to vote for a United Nations resolution condemning the Soviet invasion of Afghanistan. And while claiming the need to preserve a mixed economy, they were tightening controls over business, obsessed as they were with the need for the state to control the means of production.[3] As for political pluralism, the Sandinistas began to impose press censorship and prohibit opposition political rallies. They set up a so-called popular church composed of clergymen who supported the Sandinistas at a time when the official hierarchy of the Roman Catholic Church, which had supported the revolution, was becoming increasingly critical of the government's Marxist-Leninist line. In 1982 they also suspended the right of habeas corpus.

Although the regime officially recognized non-Sandinista trade unions, the Sandinistas also continued to bring these unions under their control. In 1980 they set up the Sandinista Workers Federation, which joined the Soviet-controlled World Federation of Trade Unions. Since then the Sandinistas have repeatedly tried to intimidate leaders of the Social Democrats and church-backed unions; in June 1983, for example, leaders of the longshoremen's union were reportedly arrested while discussing a plan to leave the federation and join the Social Democratic group.

During this period the U.S. government never seriously entertained the possibility that a different approach might produce a different result—for example, less dependence on Cuba. Instead, Washington cut economic aid, eliminated the sugar quota and finally mounted a "secret war" in which the CIA armed Nicaraguan exiles in neighboring Honduras to harass and, it was hoped, to overthrow the government in Managua. Many of the original counterrevolutionaries *(contras)* were drawn from Somoza's brutal National Guard, the least promising group to support if the United States wanted to promote a democratic alternative to the Sandinistas.

In contrast to what was happening in Nicaragua, in

1981 El Salvador briefly appeared as a promising terrain for countering revolution through an enlargement of political participation. When a guerrilla offensive failed, however, the Reagan Administration did not seize the opportunity for negotiations with the rebel front this development might have offered, but instead backed a policy of total military victory. Once again, a military rather than a diplomatic solution was chosen, and when the Salvadoran army showed itself ill-suited to win any such victory, more training in the United States or by U.S. officers based in Honduras was once again held to promise success. More money, too. U.S. military aid to El Salvador came to $6 million in 1980; it reached $65 million in fiscal 1984.

Further evidence of the unwillingness of the Reagan Administration to explore available paths of negotiation came in the summer of 1983. On July 17 the presidents of four Latin American countries—Mexico, Venezuela, Colombia and Panama, the so-called Contadora group—urged immediate negotiations to arrest "the rapid deterioration" of the situation in Central America. Included in their program was a call for the removal of all foreign military bases and advisers—and a trade-off between the withdrawal of Cubans in Nicaragua and the departure of U.S. advisers in El Salvador and the U.S. training units in Honduras. They also called for a freeze on arms shipments to and among the countries of the region and said they would require every Central American state not to interfere in the affairs of another. Presumably, this meant that Nicaragua would have to cut off supplying arms to El Salvador, while Honduras and Costa Rica would curb the activities of the counterrevolutionary groups operating from their territories.[4] In response to the Contadora group's proposals, which were further elaborated in a twenty-one-point "Declaration of Objectives" in October 1983, Castro said that he could be counted on for "negotiable solutions." He then stated publicly that Cuba would stop all military aid to Nicaragua if an agreement could be reached for "all countries not to send arms and advisers to Central America."[5]

Finally, on July 19, 1983, the fourth anniversary of the Nicaraguan revolution, the Nicaraguan government also announced that it was willing to participate in international talks to achieve peace in the region, and called for an "absolute end to all arms supplies by any country to the parties in El Salvador"—a tacit recognition that Nicaragua had indeed been supplying the guerrillas there. The Reagan Administration, in turn, claimed that it welcomed the Nicaraguan initiative. But nothing happened. The Contadora group's proposals were overshadowed by Reagan's decision to send the fleet to maneuver in waters off Central America. Moreover, the President declared that "all the American states" might provide a better forum for finding a negotiated settlement to the problems of Central America than the four nations making up the Contadora group.[6]

The purposes underlying the Administration's apparent diplomatic disinterest, if they were ever truly in question, became clearer when Under Secretary of Defense for Policy Fred Iklé addressed the Baltimore Council on Foreign Affairs on September 12. Mr. Iklé saw Nicaragua as "more dangerous than Castro's Cuba, since it shares hard-to-find borders with Honduras and Costa Rica." For this reason he urged Congress to endorse U.S. support for the "democratic resistance forces in Nicaragua" that are trying to overthrow the Sandinista regime. Even if the guerrillas in El Salvador were brought under control, "the only way to help protect the democracies might be for the United States to place forward deployed forces in these countries, as in Korea or West Germany." In short, if we cannot "prevent consolidation of a Sandinista regime in Nicaragua that would become an arsenal for insurgency, a safe haven for the export of violence . . . we have to anticipate the partition of Central America. Such a development would then force us to man a new military front-line of the East-West conflict right here on our continent."

From this point of view, very little business can usefully be done with the Sandinistas—or with the guerrilla front in El Salvador. Nor, as it turns out, is there much to be gained from dealing with Cuba, "a Soviet surrogate." To the Reagan Administration, the path to negotiations has always seemed unpropitious: in October 1981, when the revolutionary spokesmen in El Salvador offered to negotiate "without preconditions," nothing came of it; when the Sandinistas responded positively to Administration proposals in the spring of 1982, an Administration official said they were merely "playing games."[7] Small wonder, then, that the proposals of the Contadora group should be ignored. For negotiations, far from being a fruitless or frustrating experience for the Reagan Administration, have never been seriously considered.

As 1983 came to an end, the Sandinistas came up with a new series of peace proposals in four draft treaties —nonaggression pacts between Nicaragua and Honduras, and between Nicaragua and the United States, a broader nonaggression treaty to be signed by all the Central American governments, and "a draft accord to contribute to the peaceful solution of the armed conflict in the Republic of El Salvador." The Contadora countries were asked to act as guarantors of the treaties.

In the treaties, Nicaragua proposed that military aid and "the supply and trafficking of arms, munitions and military equipment" to contending forces in El Salvador and Nicaragua be suspended. The treaties would also permit on-site inspections in Nicaragua and the other Central American countries. Washington refused to discuss the proposed accords, saying that they should be submitted to the Contadora group.[8]

The Sandinistas then took some conciliatory steps. They asked Salvadoran rebel leaders to leave the country, eased press censorship, prepared a schedule for elections in 1985 (since moved up to late 1984), offered guarantees to businessmen, and conferred with leaders of the Church who had been critical of the Leninist direction of the regime. Most significant of all from an international standpoint, they ordered 1,000

Cuban military advisers to leave the country, in addition to a group of 1,200 Cuban teachers and technicians. These moves were made as fears of a U.S. invasion grew after Washington's intervention in Grenada. But the Sandinistas were also under pressure from the socialist governments of Western Europe, as well as from Mexico and Venezuela, to adopt more pluralistic policies.[9]

The Reagan Administration showed no inclination to take the new approaches seriously. It appeared to see the concessions as purely tactical and temporary, to gain time in order to consolidate the revolution.[10] As the United States entered its election year, it became clearer than ever that the Administration would be satisfied with nothing less than a radical change of regime; its concern was not to quarantine Nicaragua but rather to eliminate the Marxist direction of the Sandinistas.

Under pressure from the new Mexican president, Miguel de la Madrid, however, the Administration dispatched Secretary of State George Schulz to Managua in June to meet with the leader of the Nicaraguan junta. This was to be the first in a series of high-level talks designed to last until the American presidential election. The Administration declared that this meeting represented no substantial policy change.

Despite the seriousness of the Nicaraguan situation, the Reagan Administration has consistently found the situation in El Salvador the most perilous, and the prospects for a peaceful outcome dimmest. In March 1982 the United States sponsored an election in that country. It produced a grotesque outcome, with the extreme right holding the balance of power, and although Washington pressured the military to install a moderate conservative as president, the longstanding realities of power in El Salvador meant that the United States has had to deal almost exclusively with the military forces in seeking any solution to the conflict. Indeed, the Administration has chosen a strategy of training new cadres of young officers who will, it hopes, institute democratic reforms while fighting ever more vigorously to destroy the guerrillas. By expanding the officer corps from about 400 in the 1970s to slightly more than 2,000, Washington hopes to break the intimate connection between the oligarchs and the officers. Once again ignoring history, Reagan and his advisers fail to understand that the probable result of such a policy (as demonstrated time and again in the history of the five states, perhaps most notably in the case of Nicaragua's National Guard) will not be the democratization of El Salvador, but the transfer of power to a new elite. This, however, was not a fundamental concern of the Reagan Administration. Without a new military caste, U.S. military commanders doubt that the Salvadoran army can win the war,[11] and it is that victory which, for Washington, is the paramount objective. With this end in mind, Salvadoran soldiers are being trained by American officers in Honduras and at Fort Benning.

By 1984 this program was not paying off. The guerrillas were on the offensive, and the American-trained soldiers were putting up a poor show, as the rebels greatly extended the contested zone. American military advisers admitted that the insurgents had met with little resistance from the army, which was hampered by low morale, poor logistical support and lack of coordination among the "sector" commanders.[12] There seemed little incentive for soldiers to fight a war once the guerrillas had adopted a policy of releasing prisoners; sons of the upper class do not serve in the army.

During most of 1983 and much of 1984, the right-wing death squads killed civilians with the connivance of the armed forces. The Salvadoran Commission on Human Rights, which works under Church auspices, claimed that 2,700 civilians were killed by death squads during the first six months of 1983. The Reagan Administration, with Congress unwilling to vote more aid unless human rights improved, began to put heavier pressure on the Salvadoran military to take action against those involved in the assassinations. Finally the Salvadoran army transferred abroad two former officers said to be connected with the killings. Yet according to Robert White, the former U.S. ambassador to El Salvador, "men responsible for civilian murders still staff intelligence sections, head military garrisons and lead American-trained units accused of massacres in rural regions."[13] Recent evidence bears out these statements—a former Salvadoran military official, speaking anonymously and from the safety of refuge in the southern United States, has given members of the U.S. Congress information as to the organization and workings of the Salvadoran death squads, in exchange for monetary compensation and guarantees of his personal safety. His statements tie the squads directly to high-ranking government officials, including former Minister of Defense José Guillermo Garciá, his successor, Eugenio Vides Casanova, Treasury Police Chief Colonel Nicolás Carranza (transferred out of the country after the spring 1984 presidential elections) and Roberto d'Aubuisson, leader of the far-right Nationalist Republican Alliance (ARENA).[14] Despite such reports, only five death squad members have been convicted of any of the more than 20,000 killings of civilians by right-wing groups that have taken place during the last few years. Yet Reagan's Secretary of State, George Shultz, felt satisfied enough with the Salvadoran situation to have announced, on January 31, 1984, that the government of Alvaro Magaña was making "considerable" progress on human rights, calling the government's performance "a very good record."[15] Such statements were clearly devised to persuade Congress and the American public to endorse the Reagan Administration's true goal: eradicating the existence of, or possibility for, Marxist-Leninist states in the region.

The history of U.S.–Central American relations demonstrates, vividly and repeatedly, that the policies now being pursued by the Reagan Administration are neither original nor likely to succeed. The President and his advisers, however, have shown as little interest in heeding such historical warnings as they have in pursuing negotiations. By emphasizing ideological purity rather than the need for workable security guarantees, and by having abandoned diplomacy for military actions, the United States has made it virtually impossible to disentangle itself militarily from the region. Even the best-intentioned Administration—and there is no evidence that the Democrats offer a significant alternative to the over-all strategy that has been pursued—will find the task of withdrawal and reconciliation enormously hard to accomplish.

2

Throughout the early years of Ronald Reagan's term as President, the argument was being made (as it had been before and would be again) that withdrawal, even from a country where our allies were murdering civilians and were ineffectual in dealing with the enemy, would bring American "credibility" into question; therefore the war must go on. Certainly this was the overriding concern of Reagan's Administration. But it is an argument that has not been universally accepted in the United States, and Washington's pursuit of a flagrant militarization of the region had, by the spring of 1983, caused the Central American debate to be thrust once again into the center of U.S. national affairs.

Moreover, with a presidential election campaign coming up in just under a year, the Reagan Administration felt the need to demonstrate its willingness to take a more open view of the Central American situation than it had yet been credited with. In addition, there was the desire to silence critics who claimed that President Reagan, in Central America as in other parts of the world, had no clearly defined, long-term foreign policy that amounted to much more than the exercise of American military strength. Under this reasoning, Reagan and his advisers came up with the idea of a bipartisan commission on Central America, to be made up of leading members of America's political, business and academic communities. The commission was to be headed by former Secretary of State Henry Kissinger and was to submit its findings directly to the President by the end of the year. Reagan pledged that he would give serious weight to the advice of the commissioners.

There can be little doubt that the report of the National Bipartisan Commission on Central America was the single most significant document on U.S.–Central American relations ever to have appeared. The varied backgrounds and occupations of the commissioners, and the highly public manner in which their investigation was conducted and their report submitted, all suggested that many, if not most, citizens of the United States were and are anxious that some sort of progress be made in settling Central America's endless war. Because of this and because so many of the problems dealt with in the report are still very much with us today, an examination of the commission's findings is necessary in any serious consideration of U.S.–Central American relations.

What was most striking about the report was its contradictions. On the one hand, the commission saw Nicaragua as the implacably dangerous arm of Soviet and Cuban power and El Salvador as mainly threatened by outside forces. From this one might conclude that negotiations with the Nicaraguan government or the Salvadoran opposition would be doomed from the start and that only military pressure would be able to advance American interests. On the other hand, the report recommended a series of negotiations with the Sandinistas that, if seriously pursued, might yet help bring peace to the region.

The main weakness of the report, however, was its insistence on staking the "credibility" of the United States itself on a desirable outcome in two small, weak and poor countries in Central America. If Washington were to permit the existence of a Marxist regime, as in Nicaragua, or abandon El Salvador to its own devices, then, according to the report, the United States would seem to lack the power to control its own sphere of influence, a grave threat to the "global balance of power." Here the report reflected the view of President Reagan in his address to a joint session of Congress, April 27, 1983: "If we cannot defend ourselves there [in Central America], we cannot expect to prevail elsewhere. Our credibility would collapse, our alliances would crumble. . . ." Perceptions of credibility depend on the subjective judgment of others. The Kissinger report ended by describing a situation in which U.S. behavior would be seen by ourselves, and therefore others, as leading to a major victory or a major defeat—even though, as we shall see, the report never made clear what major U.S. interests are directly at stake in Central America.

The tone of the report was remarkably similar to the Rockefeller report of 1969. It is as if those who drafted the recommendations had ignored the history of the region before, during and after Rockefeller's mission. Once again the United States was to depend on the Central American military to carry out its proposals; the officers we have backed were again seen as the engines of reform.[16] The vast amount of economic aid suggested—$8.4 billion over five years—was to help promote democratic change in countries where democracy (except for Costa Rica, a sound democracy which has no army) scarcely exists. In stressing the need to maintain the balance of power with the Soviet Union, the panel also urged a "significantly larger program of military assistance."[17] The Pentagon, the panel observed, had estimated that $400 million would be needed for El Salvador in 1984 and 1985—more than triple the present level—in order to protect Central America from falling under the sway of the Soviet Union. The panel apparently accepted this estimate unquestioningly, without scrutinizing the military forces that would receive the money or asking how effectively it would be spent.

Much the same could be said for the recommendations to increase economic aid to the seven countries of the region—the report added Belize and Panama to the traditional list of five—by adding $400 million to the already appropriated U.S. funds for fiscal 1984 of $477 million. The $8 billion to be spent between 1985 and 1990 was to be "a rough doubling of U.S. economic assistance from the 1983 level." Just how it should be used to relieve the poverty that continues to "plague most of the region's people," as the report puts it, was left unclear. The panel recommended that the United States "review non-tariff barriers to imports from Central America by other major trading countries." In a dissenting note, the economist Carlos Díaz-Alejandro criticized the report for its "timidity" in "recommending a further opening of the U.S. market to Central American exports," which "sharply contrasts with statements about the strategic importance of that region to the U.S."

True, the report was careful to point out that "unless economic recovery is accompanied by social progress and political reform, additional financial support will ultimately be wasted. By the same token, without recovery, the political and security prospects will be grim." But characteristically, it did not say how social progress and political reform might be expected to take place in El Salvador, where progress on land reform has been consistently delayed, where labor leaders are threatened by death squads, and where the upper 20 percent of the population holds 66 percent of the total income and the bottom 50 percent of the population has only 12 percent—"the most skewed income distribution in all of Central America."[18]

Moreover, in El Salvador the government is controlled by the armed forces, in Honduras it is dominated by them, in Guatemala run by them. (Indeed, the report charged that in Guatemala the security forces have, in the cities, "murdered those even suspected of dissent"; and in the countryside, "they have at times killed indiscriminately.") If a country has democratic political processes, the money is more likely to be budgeted in response to the local needs as reflected in popular demands. Otherwise, there is every reason to expect a recurrence of the inequities of the 1960s when aid and a booming world economy did not, as the report made clear, produce more equitable societies. Except for Costa Rica, there is no truly democratic government in Central America. Whether the money ends up largely in the hands of oligarchs or bureaucrats, it is unlikely to be of great benefit to the citizens of these unhappy countries, but it is very likely to reinforce the status quo. This probability was not confronted in the report.

The heart of the Kissinger report was a discussion of Central American security issues. The message here was clear: unless vigorous military measures are taken to prevent El Salvador from falling to the guerrillas, and unless Nicaragua changes its internal structure, then economic and social progress in the region is doomed. Win the war, this time in El Salvador, the report argued, because democracy can only flourish in the absence of threat. "Unless checked, the insurgents can destroy faster than the reformers can build," the panel declared, because "once the lines of external support are in place, [the insurgency] has a momentum which reforms alone cannot stop."

Here again Latin American history could have been instructive. In Venezuela during the late 1950s and early 1960s, the guerrillas were beaten because a reformist government was in power. There is little hard evidence that a war can be won by repressive governments (and whatever the left-of-center leanings of President Duarte, the military remains the decisive voice in Salvadoran affairs) unless they embark on a draconian course of extermination, something that the panel did not recommend and that would surely receive no support from the American public. And even then, the "victory" is likely to be temporary, while the insurgency continues, as has been the case in Guatemala.

The section on security issues described an insurgency in El Salvador that "not only opposes democracy and is committed to the violent seizure of power, but also threatens U.S. security interests because of its ties to Nicaragua, Cuba, and the Soviet Union." The report contained much useful information on Cuba's aid to the guerrillas, and no one can doubt that the Cubans continue to have influence among the Sandinista and FMLN leaders. But nowhere did the report say exactly how U.S. security interests are threatened. At one point it specifically disavowed any notion that a Soviet base would be "the sole, or even the major, threat to U.S. interests." The threat seemed to derive mostly from the possibility that Washington will fail to show itself firmly in control of its sphere of influence. "The ability of the United States to sustain a tolerable balance of power on the global scene," the report argued, "depends on the inherent security of its land borders." By feeling secure at home, the United States could afford to maintain its alliances in Europe and the Far East. Thus, if the Soviet Union and its ally Cuba were to advance their "power on the American mainland," this would affect "the global balance. To the extent that a further Marxist-Leninist advance in Central America . . . required us to defend against security threats near our borders, we would face a difficult choice between unpalatable alternatives. We would either have to assume a permanently increased defense burden, or see our capacity to defend distant troublespots reduced. . . . From the stand-point of the Soviet Union, it would be a major strategic coup to impose on the United States the burden of defending our southern approaches."

The panel went on to cite the threat to the Panama Canal, and the danger of refugees, "perhaps millions of them, many of whom would seek entry into the United States." In short, "the crisis is on our doorstep." Then came the telling phrase: "our credibility worldwide is engaged." The "triumph of hostile forces in what the Soviets call the 'strategic rear' of the United States would be read as a sign of U.S. impotence." If America were to be perceived as a pitiful, helpless giant, as Richard Nixon once feared, then, the commission said, we would experience the "erosion of our power to influence events worldwide that would flow from the perception that we were unable to influence vital events close to home."

What, however, is the precise security threat "on our doorstep?" The commission did not say. Mexico, the most important domino, does not profess itself threatened by events in small Central American countries. The Soviets installed in Cuba can already threaten our sea lanes, as the panel pointed out, and we have been able to live with this for twenty years. Add to all this the fact that nuclear submarines—each a highly mobile and concealed "base" of significant power—have come to play an increasingly large role in the international security forces of both the United States and the Soviet Union, and the value to the Soviets of an open and obvious strategic base in Central America becomes even more difficult to imagine.

As in the case of the British Empire during the last century, the *actual* threat to the security of the United States in Central America is hard to find beneath all the talk of the *supposed* ambitions of a rival power.

Here the recent study by the Carnegie Endowment for International Peace, an independent, Washington-based organization of political and economic analysts, provides the careful analysis of Central American security issues that the Kissinger panel did not undertake. We are reminded, in respect to the Salvadoran military, that "security depends on the popular perception that the military serves national rather than class interests, that it defends rather than abuses individual rights."[19] This explains why many of El Salvador's citizens do not feel protected by their own security forces. During the last three and a half years, Congress has made military aid to El Salvador contingent on the President's certifying progress on human rights—which was done again and again with no discernible progress. Greater firepower resulted in no greater sense of civic responsibility.

As for Soviet behavior, the Carnegie study makes careful distinctions between actual and potential Soviet threats. It points out that "the real problem" is the possibility that Soviet "military facilities might be established in the wake of Soviet-aligned guerrilla victories." Even though Nicaragua has expanded its army of 50,000 (including 25,000 reserves), its military capacities are largely defensive. Should the Sandinistas try to invade Honduras, for example, the odds heavily favor Honduras, whose air force could easily blunt any armored thrust through the flatland along the Gulf of Fonseca. Since Cuba already poses a threat to U.S. sea lines of communication, the serious additional threats in Central America would be the emplacement of Soviet offensive weapons, such as MiG-23s, or an invasion by Cuba or Nicaragua of its neighbors.

In both cases the United States could—and, in my view, should—make clear that it would respond with air power and combat troops if necessary; under these circumstances military action would be highly unlikely but would undoubtedly be supported by the Congress and the public if U.S. conditions were violated. In Nicaragua today, the Carnegie study points out, "the legitimate security concerns of both [the United States and Nicaragua] might be addressed by a policy which combined a credible threat of U.S. retaliation if Soviet offensive weapons were introduced, with a U.S. pledge not to invade Nicaragua." This suggests a negotiation that would be well worth considering, one that was not brought up in the Kissinger report.

Instead of stressing the need to negotiate regional security guarantees with Nicaragua, the Kissinger panel seemed, in some of its language, simply to rule out tolerating a Marxist-Leninist regime there. This was so not only because "Nicaragua is tied into the Cuban, and thereby the Soviet, intelligence network" but also because their neighbors expressed "deep foreboding about the impact of a militarized totalitarian Nicaragua on the peace and security of the region." But containment of Nicaragua was viewed as impossible: "To contain the export of revolution would require a level of vigilance and sustained effort that would be difficult for Nicaragua's neighbors and even for the United States." A long-term containment, the panel concluded, would require U.S. military power backing up local forces of "stable allies." Given these premises, says the Kissinger commission's report, Nicaraguan peace initiatives "have given little cause for optimism that we could move toward [the] objectives" of the Contadora group—which, let us remember, called for linking security in the region to the increase of democracy in its various countries.

Still, having described the Nicaraguan regime as menacing and implacable, in language close to that of the Reagan Administration, the Kissinger report— again somewhat contradictorily—recommended that "whatever the prospects seem to be for productive negotiations, the United States must spare no effort to pursue the diplomatic route. Nicaragua's willingness to enter into a general agreement should be thoroughly tested through negotiations and actions. . . . Every avenue should be explored to see if the vague signals emanating from Managua in recent weeks can be translated into concrete progress." Such exploration is precisely what the Reagan Administration has always refused to undertake, but nowhere did the Kissinger report make a careful analysis of the Nicaraguan draft treaties I have already mentioned. It did not make clear what proposals could or could not be thoroughly tested.

As for U.S. support for the Nicaraguan insurgents based in Honduras, a majority of the members of the commission were cited as believing that the covert war was "one of the incentives working in favor of a negotiated settlement." But the commission made no judgment "on whether, or how, the States should provide support for these insurgent forces." Moreover, two members—Henry Cisneros, mayor of San Antonio, Texas, and Carlos Díaz-Alejandro—in dissenting notes were highly critical of the covert aid Washington was giving and continues to give to the *contras.* Far from being an incentive to democratization, the covert war, in Díaz-Alejandro's words, "is more likely to strengthen the most extremist sectors of the Sandinista leadership." The report itself did not consider or reply to this argument.

Toward El Salvador, too, the panel followed an inconsistent line. It ruled out any explicit concept of power-sharing between the government and the guerrillas, or, more accurately, between the official Salvadoran armed forces and the guerrillas. The panel believed that any such notion would mean delivering the government over to the guerrillas. But as things stand now, power-sharing has for some time been little more than wishful thinking. The current military leaders would never agree to it, and it is hard to imagine any amount of U.S. pressure that would force them to. It was quite clear in my own discussions with the military and other Salvadorans in October 1983 that both power-sharing and serious reform were conceivable only if the upper ranks of the military were no longer in charge.[20] As a "leading spokesman" for the Roman Catholic Archdiocese in San Salvador put it on January 28, 1984, "To clean things up would require a total change in the military structure, which is something that neither the government nor even the Americans are ready to do."[21]

The commission, however, recommended that money be supplied only to shore up the existing military structure. The problem for the Salvadorans, the report recognized, has consistently been both the external support the rebels have received and "the brutal methods practiced by certain reactionary forces in Central America," i.e., the death squads. Curing El Salvador's ills therefore would require a new infusion of military aid as well as encouraging the government to curb the death squads. A successful counterinsurgency effort along American lines, which would also mean action on the "economic and social fronts," is required before anyone can seek a political solution. In the security section of the report, then, the panel was quite clear in asserting that victory comes first, negotiations later. The already-mentioned $400 million in U.S. military aid in 1984 and 1985 would be needed just "to break the military stalemate." (Within a week after the report was released, the Reagan Administration asked for almost precisely this amount, while the Salvadoran army was reported planning to expand its overall troop strength by 20 percent.[22])

But here the panel ran into one of its deepest contradictions. It also insisted that any military aid be contingent on "demonstrated progress" toward free elections, an effective judicial system and the ending of the activities of the death squads, and that these conditions be "seriously enforced." It even stated that, over time, elections could not succeed unless the Salvadoran government were to provide "basic security for teachers, editors and writers, labor and religious opinion," and a "secure environment" for all those who might wish to take part in the elections, including "leftists" and "centrists." The U.S. government "must insist that these conditions be met." But what if the security forces themselves are not in the least interested in protecting such people and such political forces but, on the contrary, prefer to continue killing and terrorizing them as they have done in the past? On this critical question the report was silent. Only Kissinger himself and two other commissioners answered it in a dissenting note, recording their "strong view that neither the Congress nor the Executive Branch interpret conditionality in a manner that leads to a Marxist-Leninist victory" in El Salvador. But the smallness of the dissenting group left both the report's conditions for continuing military aid and its contradictions standing.

What alternatives might the commission have considered? If the United States were able to reorganize the armed forces by relieving the upper ranks of their commands, then, perhaps, the military might try to end the violence directed against any presumed opponents and so increase its support among the population. In this case, it might be possible to split the guerrilla fronts and form a government that would not only be able to share power but even find widespread popular backing. This possibility, an increasingly slim one, the commission never explored; indeed, the notion of looking for and exploiting different tendencies in the Salvadoran guerrilla front never came up in the body of the report. It appeared only in the dissent of Henry Cisneros, who recognized that there are moderates in the FDR (Democratic Revolutionary Front)–FMLN guerrilla movement who might be persuaded to take part in talks "to determine the extent to which meaningful dialogue on coalition approaches and structural reforms can proceed."

Instead, the panel clung to its preference for elections and concentrated on urging that they be free, fair and protected. It held open the possibility of a kind of power-sharing when it suggested that the government that was to be elected in the spring of 1984 invite the guerrilla front to take part in a commission to organize the municipal elections of 1985. But it hardly seems realistic that the present government, wholly dependent on the armed forces to guarantee its continued existence, will invite the insurgents to take part in "security arrangements." The commission seemed to assume that the Salvadoran politicians and military men would act like well-intentioned democrats; little in their recent record bears out such hopes and a great deal contradicts them. All this, however, is of small concern to the Reagan Administration, which will, we may expect, continue to use the Kissinger commission's warnings on "security" to grind down support in Congress for its stand on human rights.

PART
III

1

In the spring of 1982, when I returned from a lengthy trip to Central America, I felt that there was a reasonable chance for a series of negotiations—between Washington and Managua; between Washington and Havana; and between the contending forces in El Salvador—that could bring about an overall peace settlement.[1] Since then, that opportunity has been effectively closed off by the Reagan Administration's single-minded devotion to military solutions.

In late 1983 I again visited the region, as well as Mexico and Cuba, and before and during my trip again spoke with high officials both in and out of government. These included the Mexican foreign minister, Bernardo Sepúlveda; Cuba's vice president and deputy prime minister, Carlos Rafael Rodríguez, and deputy foreign minister, Ricardo Alarcón; El Salvador's then-president, Alvaro Magaña; Honduras' then–commander in chief, General Gustavo Álvarez Martinez; and numerous Sandinista officials and military men as well as leaders of the Nicaraguan exile forces located in Honduras. In addition, I had extensive conversations with U.S. military and diplomatic representatives and visited the contested zones along the Nicaragua-Honduras border.

.   .   .

As the most important power in the region, Mexico is an invaluable starting point for any analysis of the turmoil in Central America. Fearing unrest that might spill over into a wider war, the Mexicans have taken the lead over the past two years in seeking negotiated solutions to the tensions between Washington and Managua and, more generally, in searching for an alternative to the militarization of the region. In particular, Mexico wants peace on its southern border where Guatemalan guerrillas are fighting against the authoritarian and brutally repressive regime of General Oscar Mejía Victores and using Mexican territory as a haven. In any case, Mexican intellectuals and government officials—including those most hostile to Marxism—do not believe that Mexico will turn out to be "the last domino," as the Reagan Administration fears, even if Marxist-Leninist states come to power in El Salvador and Nicaragua. As the Mexican Foreign Office put it in 1984, "We must repeat that Mexico has already had its revolution, in 1910, which it fought to change the economic and social structure of the country. Central America is fighting now for what Mexico has already fought for, and this is the difference between the Mexican reality and the Central American revolution."[2]

Ideology is not something Mexicans are much concerned about. Indeed, the ability of the Institutional Revolutionary Party (PRI), Mexico's ruling party, to co-opt its opponents is a continuing wonder in Mexican political life, undiminished by current economic adversity—the 90 percent inflation and high unemployment that have resulted from Mexico's staggering external debt. As the Mexicans point out, the PRI was founded on the ideology of revolution and has become a party of the status quo, with an enormous bureaucracy to support the system of state capitalism that now exists. The Mexican experience at first persuaded the former president, José López Portillo, that the Sandinista revolution could take a non-Marxist path. Now the Mexican officials I talked to are not so sure. The Sandinistas, they observed, seem more strongly drawn to the Cuban model of a centralized Leninist state than to the Mexican political pattern.

Under the administration of Miguel de la Madrid, the broad outlines of Mexican foreign policy remain largely unchanged, but there is a marked difference in emphasis. Whereas the previous administration seemed to want to displace U.S. predominance in Central America, the new president stresses the traditional Mexican position of nonintervention. When asked, for example, why Mexico never tried to take the place of the Cubans in Nicaragua, many of whom (whatever their paramilitary duties may have been) were teachers and medical personnel, the foreign minister said flatly that Mexico had had no intention of sending any advisers there. Thus Mexico finds itself in a dilemma: while it views with concern such processes as the "Cubanization" of Nicaragua, it remains unwilling to be directly involved, preferring to rest comfortably on its principles.

From intellectuals like Carlos Fuentes and Octavio Paz, I heard the same note of caution when we spoke of Mexican involvement in Central America. As Fuentes explains it, the antimilitary tradition in Mexico means that it is unlikely that Mexico could ever send troops into Central America, even as part of a peacekeeping force. Paz agrees with Fuentes, but he regrets Mexico's "isolationism" and the government's refusal to see the danger to Central America, and even to Mexico itself, should there be a series of Soviet-aligned Communist regimes in the region, something Paz frankly fears. By remaining aloof from the Nicaraguan revolution, Paz pointed out, Mexico did not help the non-Marxist democratic forces represented by such figures as Arturo Cruz, the former head of the Central Bank, after the revolution. As Paz himself wrote in *The Labyrinth of Solitude,* "The Mexican is always remote from the world and from other people. And also from himself."

Unable and certainly unwilling to act by itself, Mexico has sought support from the other powers of the region. Venezuela had already aligned its policy with Mexico's in urging negotiations among the warring factions in El Salvador after the spring 1982 elections, when Venezuela's candidate, the Christian Democrat José Napoleón Duarte, was forced out of office. Soon Mexico looked for wider support and managed to get it with the formation of the Contadora group. As stated earlier, the group initially proposed to separate security issues in Central America from considerations of internal developments (such as the promotion of the democratic process), but then, in its October 1983 "Declaration of Objectives," urged governments "to adopt measures leading to the establishment or in some cases the perfecting of democratic, representative and pluralistic systems."[3]

While it is true that the Reagan Administration was at first hostile to the Contadora group, preferring that any mediation include other Latin American states that might not be so averse to Washington's emphasis on military solutions to political problems, it is also true that by the fall of 1983, Washington had come to embrace Contadora, if only rhetorically. There were two reasons for this shift: first, Washington wished to display at least the appearance of a willingness to consider peaceful solutions to both the continuing war in El Salvador and Nicaragua's support for leftist guerrilla movements. But more important, as a senior American diplomat in Central America explained to me, the Reagan Administration soon found Contadora useful as a way of avoiding negotiations; Washington could simply put aside any serious consideration of bilateral approaches that it did not want to pursue by insisting that they be submitted to Contadora. Like the United Nations in its early years, Contadora is universally praised but it is impotent, and it can become a useful mechanism for settling Central American disputes only if the United States is honestly prepared to employ it.

Unlike the Mexican officials, the Cuban leaders I talked to harbored no apparent doubts about their global vocation. Committed to "internationalism" and solidarity with revolutionary movements abroad, the Cuban leaders look to their foreign policy to provide them with successes that have been singularly lacking on the domestic front. By sending overseas about 35,000 troops (from its active-duty forces of 225,000), most of them to Angola and Ethiopia, as well as military advisers to Nicaragua, Grenada and even as far as South Yemen, Cuba has extended its influence even though this costs the country dearly. Officially, Cuba's overall debt, in both hard and soft currencies, reached more than $12 billion in 1982, and its imports regularly exceed its exports. Soviet economic aid helps to underwrite Cuba's foreign involvements, though it is fair to point out that substantial Soviet economic aid was forthcoming well before the Cubans sent troops overseas in the mid-1970s. Since 1961 Cuba has received more than $30 billion in economic aid from the U.S.S.R.; in 1982 this aid came to more than 25 percent of Cuba's gross national product —all this apart from any military assistance.[4]

Most Soviet assistance to Cuba is, of course, military aid, which increased after Reagan's election and the subsequent sharpening of Washington's anti-Cuban rhetoric. It is unclear, however, what share of such military equipment has been sent on to Central America. My conversations with Cuban leaders, and with diplomats who are in touch with them, suggested a deep reluctance on their part to become directly enmeshed in actual combat in the region. This attitude derives both from a realistic acceptance of the overwhelming U.S. military strength in the region and continued awareness of Cuba's vulnerability, and from a fear that the Reagan Administration may seize any provocation to invade the island itself.

Cuban leaders insist that their military assistance to El Salvador's rebels has been significantly cut back. In our conversations, they concentrated on possible political solutions, such as power-sharing between the guerrillas and the Salvadoran armed forces and support for the Nicaraguan six-point program of July 1983. Castro himself characterized this as a "willingness to sign a nonaggression pact with Honduras and a willingness to reach an agreement on the issue of El Salvador based on an end to all provision of weapons to the contending parties."[5] The U.S. invasion of Grenada has doubtless strengthened Cuba's desire for negotiations in Central America; indeed, Castro acknowledged after the Grenada episode that he could not help Nicaragua if it were attacked by U.S. forces.[6]

As the Cuban leaders see it, the situation of the guerrillas has improved in El Salvador despite the failure of the "final offensive" in early 1981. In large part, they said, the reason for this improvement is that the five guerrilla organizations that make up the FMLN have finally coordinated their political and military tactics. They added that the guerrillas did so because they listened to Cuba's advice and then followed it. This analysis of the FMLN was later confirmed by the American military and political officers I talked to in El Salvador. (However, a small splinter group broke off from the front in the fall of 1983 and has since committed sporadic acts of urban terrorism.)

The very success of the guerrillas, the Cubans told me, makes an arrangement for power-sharing desirable, although this would necessarily retard the development of El Salvador into a Marxist-Leninist state; in El Salvador's case, "radical socialism in the short term is impossible." They point out that the proximity of El Salvador to the United States, the existence of a middle class, and the difficult economic situation of the Soviet bloc call for different tactics for eventually converting El Salvador into a Communist state. The Cubans also reject any other way of allowing the guerrillas to participate in the existing government. They claim that the safety of the guerrillas could not be guaranteed if, as the U.S. government has proposed, they were to participate in elections. Although the Cuban leaders had talked in 1982 of the possibility of introducing peacekeeping forces in El Salvador, they now dismiss as worthless the use of such forces, citing their impotence in the Congo in the early 1960s when Patrice Lumumba was killed.[7]

Cuba, they say, has no role in El Salvador because, unlike Nicaragua, El Salvador has "a great diversity of social classes, a broader political spectrum and is in a stage of much higher economic development." Like the Sandinistas now in power in Managua, the Cubans insist they are prepared to let the Salvadoran guerrillas fend for themselves. Unwilling to let themselves be caught out by the United States as a major arms supplier to the FMLN—which might give Washington the pretext it is looking for to intervene directly against Cuba—they appear to believe that the FMLN can hang on with the arms it captures from the government troops while it continues to press for a share of power, or even win a military victory in a long war that the United States will grow weary of supporting.

As for bilateral relations with the United States, the Cubans are willing to negotiate on issues such as the repatriation of Cuban criminals who were sent to the

United States along with other Cuban refugees in the 1980 Mariel boatlift—but only if these issues are tied to the broader range of U.S.-Cuban relations. They showed no disposition to modify any of Cuba's significant foreign policy involvements in Angola or elsewhere in Africa. The Cubans themselves feel cut off from any approaches from Washington since the resignation of Alexander Haig as Secretary of State in the summer of 1982. As the Cubans tell it, the meeting Carlos Rafael Rodríguez had with Secretary Haig in Mexico City in November 1981 was encouraging simply because it took place at all. But the second meeting, with Reagan's envoy General Vernon Walters, in Havana in February 1982, got nowhere. As the Cuban deputy prime minister put it: "It was not a dialogue." Instead, it was a virtual monologue, "full of anecdotes of a life which was rich in anecdotes, but which we knew."

As I left Cuba for Central America I saw no hope for a serious dialogue between Washington and Havana. Cuba might be willing to put distance between itself and the fighting in El Salvador, but the United States, for its part, would negotiate with Cuba only if Havana renounced its policy of supporting armed revolution elsewhere, which the Cubans are not prepared to do. Meanwhile, after the Grenada intervention, the possibility of military confrontation with Cuba may have increased.

Visiting Honduras after Cuba, one comes to understand why a wider regional conflict in Central America is more and more likely. It is in Honduras, after all, that many of the exiles who oppose the Sandinistas and are backed by the CIA are based. These *contras,* still made up in part of many former supporters of the hated Somoza, now also include a number of former supporters of the Nicaraguan revolution who have become disenchanted by the Marxist direction it has been taking. The Nicaraguan Democratic Force, or FDN, as the nationalist movement calls itself, has held negotiations with the other group of exiles fighting the Sandinistas, the Democratic Revolutionary Alliance, or ARDE, based in Costa Rica. Coordinated operations by the two groups, estimated at about 10,000 men, would present the Nicaraguan regime with a two-front war, but relations between them have always been strained. ARDE, whose military wing was headed by one of the heroes of the Sandinista revolution, Edén Pastora ("Commander Zero"), before a bomb attack seriously wounded him, and whose political half is led by Alfonso Robelo, a high school classmate of Pastora and a member of the first junta of the Sandinista government, is often split within itself. Pastora had always resisted the formation of the joint military command with the FDN called for by the CIA.[8] Unlike the FDN, ARDE sees itself as made up of "authentic Sandinistas" whose own revolution has been betrayed.

The *contras* in Honduras reject any ideas of negotiating with the Sandinistas, who, they are convinced, will spread revolution throughout Central America. "Their ultimate objective," one FDN leader told me, is "the Panama Canal and the oil fields of Mexico and

Venezuela." While the exiles claim military successes all along the Honduran-Nicaraguan border and maintain that their support within Nicaragua is increasing daily, they are also aware of their complete dependence on the United States. The CIA's financing of their so-called secret war allows them the firepower they need, but unless they are able to hold and occupy a significant portion of Nicaragua itself in the near future, they are fearful the United States will abandon them. Meanwhile, the *contras* call for free elections, a general amnesty and the "abolition of repressive institutions."

In fact, while the *contras* are considered by U.S. officials to be useful as a means of putting pressure on the Sandinistas, neither the U.S. government nor the Honduran army is convinced that they have the staying power to bring down the Nicaraguan regime. To back up the *contras* and to prepare for a successful military engagement with the Nicaraguan armed forces, the United States has resurrected, with Honduras' blessing, CONDECA, the Central American mutual defense organization, created in 1963, which includes Honduras, Guatemala, El Salvador and Panama (the northern three nations making up the self-styled "iron triangle"). Should open war with Nicaragua come, CONDECA would probably be the regional instrument used to head the campaign.

As it is, Honduras has become, in effect, America's aircraft carrier. Not only were there 3,500 American troops on joint maneuvers with the Honduran army in 1983, but the United States has also set up there the Regional Military Training Center. And there are increasing indications that Washington does not intend these to be short-term commitments: senior Reagan Administration officials have said that U.S. forces will be sent to Honduras to train in operations similar to 1983's "Big Pine" maneuvers every year for the "foreseeable future," a time that they acknowledge could be as long as twenty years.[9] And Senate investigators have indicated that "there is real evidence that our military is building airfields and other infrastructure to support a very large and possibly permanent United States military contingency there."[10]

In view of these commitments, I was not surprised to be told by the Honduran leaders that negotiating with the Sandinistas in order to ensure Honduras' security was out of the question. Although in July 1983 the Honduran government captured between 96 and 100 Honduran insurgents (which the United States says were trained in Cuba and came over the border from Nicaragua), the government's main concern is less to prevent such infiltration than to destroy the Sandinista regime and the ideology it expounds. In the president's office, in the foreign ministry and, above all, in talking with the military, I heard only one solution proposed to deal with "the ideological threat from Nicaragua." This was for Nicaragua to carry out the promises it once made to institute a mixed economy, political pluralism and nonalignment. If this were done, so the story ran, then the *contras* would be able to participate in free elections and thus the external threat to Nicaragua would be removed.

How, I asked, would Honduras arrive at this neat solution? "By putting pressure on the Sandinistas and strengthening the Honduran army." If the Nicaraguan armed forces were to attack the *contras* by crossing the Honduran border under the doctrine of "hot pursuit," then things might deteriorate to the point where "Central America will have to respond."

Under these conditions, some observers believe that Honduras' elected civilian government may be threatened. This is not likely in the near term, since the government is a feeble one and the armed forces can carry out whatever policies they prefer. For example, in May 1984 younger officers were able to force into exile General Gustavo Álvarez Martinez, the chief of the armed forces, when they came to resent his growing power and high-handed style of command. But the incipient democracy that exists in Honduras may well perish in an atmosphere of increased militarization—already there are reports, from several human rights groups, that abuses in Honduras have risen in number during the last year, and that the United States has done little or nothing to discourage the trend.[11]

Assaulted by the *contras* along its northern border, its oil tanks and pipeline damaged and its harbors mined by the rebels with the admitted help of the CIA, Nicaragua is clearly under siege. The Sandinistas insist they want and need security. And they are prepared to make important concessions to get it, even if that means cutting off remaining aid to their ideological comrades fighting in El Salvador. What they are not willing to do, they told me, is to negotiate the terms of their own rule or the direction of Nicaragua's internal affairs.

American government officials I talked to in the region are divided over the degree of support the Sandinistas enjoy. Though some concessions have been made by the Sandinistas, there remain clear signs of discontent with the direction of the revolution. Pressure on the trade unions to submit to the control of the Sandinista party is heavy and widespread; freedom to travel outside the country is more restricted; conscription began at the end of last year; the press is still censored (less so than in previous years, but censorship does remain); foreign priests who criticize the revolution have been expelled, and, despite attempts at reconciliation, many have not returned; economic shortages are common, while necessary commodities such as soap, toilet paper and gasoline are rationed. In addition, the Sandinistas have organized Cuban-style Committees to Defend Sandinism (CDS), local block associations which are used not only to carry out administrative tasks such as the distribution of supplies but also to spy on neighbors. As I was told by a leader of the CDS when I went out to see the organization at work in one of the *barrios,* "As long as there are counterrevolutionaries, we will need vigilance." The principal Sandinista leaders, particularly the powerful party organizer Bayardo Arce, I was told, are committed to the Cuban system of organizing such vigilance.

At the same time, private business still makes up about 40 percent of the economy, though prices are controlled by the state. (The government controls all banks and all access to foreign exchange and regulates all imports.) The land-reform program continues. So do ambitious efforts to improve health and education. Above all, I was told, even by Nicaraguans who are not enthusiastic about the Sandinistas, the regime receives domestic support because of the pressures—economic and military—inflicted on it by the United States as it pursues its avowed goal of forcing Nicaragua to take the road to pluralistic democracy and to move away from the direction taken by Cuba.

A trip north to the Honduran-Nicaraguan border gives some indication of the ways by which the *contras* can threaten the peace and stability of the region—and of the confidence the regime displays in the face of these adversaries. About four hours from Managua, in sparsely settled cowboy country near the small settlement of El Espino, is the main border-crossing into Honduras. After enduring repeated rebel attacks at the border, the Sandinista army has abandoned the frontier checkpoint and pulled back about five kilometers to a better defensive position. At the bottom of a high hill at the border itself, the half-dozen small buildings have been shelled and are now vacant and burned out. A hundred yards to the rear, in El Espino itself, the people have been evacuated and the houses and stores are boarded over. The new border checkpoint is now established at the Coco River, and I drove with two companions along a secondary road that ran beside the river to try to enter the town of Ocotal, which has been the scene of serious fighting.

Ocotal, with a population of about 45,000, lies on the far side of the river, surrounded by the Honduran mountains, an ideal target for mortar fire from the *contras* encamped above. The bridge has been shelled and repaired several times, and is said to be too fragile for motor traffic. I was lucky to find a jeep filled with armed militiamen to tow my Toyota sedan across the river, which was about four or five feet deep in midstream. After fording the river, we were able to drive into the town itself and found the local people heavily armed with automatic weapons.

The Sandinistas do not appear to be making use of their regular army in such places, except for the officers; instead, they depend on arming and training the militia, which is made up of local townspeople, a practice that will produce better trained civilian combat forces. That night, after a rally in the main square, trucks with uniformed militia set out for the hills where a defense perimeter of foxholes and trenches has been set up and reinforced. Throughout the night there was incessant machine-gun fire, though whether any *contras* had been engaged in direct combat was hard to tell. This may well have been "reconnaissance by fire," soldiers firing off their weapons to see if there is any response; some of the firing may have been simply to keep awake. I was told the next morning that every night was like that.

The *contras* can easily move about in this countryside, but it would be hard to imagine that they could take and hold a town of any size. The local population is busily engaged in building an elaborate network of air-raid shelters for the children and old people.

Most important, the people are armed—the clearest sign of the Sandinistas' confidence. A government will not arm a hostile population, and I was told that local militias had been given weapons in most of the country.

The rebels probably have the most support on the Atlantic coast, where the Miskito Indians are located. The Sandinistas have badly mistreated the Miskitos, herding them into relocation camps, subjecting them to a campaign of ideological reeducation. Even when Somoza exploited this area economically, he understood the need to leave the Indians alone. Failing to do so, the Sandinistas have made serious enemies.

If the *contras* could find allies among the Miskitos and other inhabitants of the east coast who have traditionally distrusted the government in Managua, then, some U.S. officials told me, a "liberated zone" (of the variety that has been seen many times on Nicaragua's east coast during the nation's history) with a provisional government might be set up that would receive diplomatic recognition from the United States and the Latin American governments it backs. Under this plan, the CONDECA countries would provide the troops to defend the provisional government; U.S. forces offshore and those based in Honduras would supply logistical support—or intervene directly if absolutely necessary.[12] This is not a prospect the more knowledgeable U.S. diplomats I talked to find attractive. They believe it risks wider war and could even include the participation of volunteers from Mexico and Venezuela fighting on the side of the Sandinistas against a U.S.-recognized "free Nicaragua."

Faced with these prospects, the Sandinistas are prepared to give security guarantees to the other countries of Central America in return for guarantees from their neighbors—and from the United States—that they need not fear for their own security. Such guarantees would give the Sandinistas time to deal with their internal problems, or, as they would put it, "to consolidate the revolution" before their elections now scheduled for the fall of this year. These ideas were embodied in the six-point program of July 1983, as well as in the four draft treaties made public toward the end of the same year.

As we have already seen, however, the Reagan Administration has consistently ignored such attempts at negotiation. By refusing even to discuss the Nicaraguan proposals, Washington has demonstrated once again its refusal to separate the question of security from its demands for internal changes—in this case, that the Sandinistas abandon their ideological commitments to make Nicaragua into a Marxist-Leninist state. In so doing, the Administration has given up on a line of negotiation that the senior American diplomats I talked to believe might yield strong benefits to both the United States and the region: no Soviet or Cuban bases on Nicaraguan soil; stopping advanced weapons systems from being imported; verification of land, sea and air bases and the border insofar as possible; and a further reduction in the number of Cuban advisers in Nicaragua.

In a very different way, the Salvadoran government is also asking the United States to guarantee its security. It expects Washington to train and equip its army until the guerrillas are exterminated or are persuaded to enter the electoral process. The Reagan Administration is finding this no easy task when confronted by a military standoff in the field and the continued violation of human rights—including the killing of thousands of civilians—by armed forces committed to the protection of their fellow citizens.

There seems little hope of serious negotiations. The FMLN has indeed followed the Cubans' advice. After the murder and suicide of two of their leaders in the spring of 1983, they coordinated their military tactics and now display far greater sophistication than they had previously shown; they are able to strike simultaneously at different targets and, according to U.S. military advisers, have taken the initiative. Moreover, the new guerrilla commander, Joaquín Villalobos, who has emerged, both militarily and politically, as the leader of the left, understands the need to offer to negotiate as well.

In their meeting in Bogotá in September 1983 with the Salvadoran Peace Commission, the FMLN delegates got nowhere with their demand that a provisional government be formed before the elections of last March. Unless there were some kind of joint military command, the rebels maintained, the Salvadoran armed forces could not guarantee their safety; indeed, when the rebel negotiators suggested that the next meeting be held in San Salvador itself, the Salvadoran Peace Commission reportedly told them that it could not undertake to protect them. To which the rebels were supposed to have replied, "If you cannot guarantee our safety for five hours, how can you guarantee it for five weeks during an election campaign?" This would have been a telling question, except that in El Salvador no one's safety can be guaranteed.

I left El Salvador convinced that power-sharing was not a realistic possibility for the government; and events since my departure have reinforced this conviction. The case for power-sharing can well be made.[13] It seems a way to end the war by having the United States compel the armed forces to guarantee the security of the rebels while we would also ensure—either on our own or by means of an international peace-keeping force—that a truly pluralistic electoral process (i.e., one involving the guerrillas) would not be manipulated. But, as demonstrated by the most recent elections in El Salvador, such a prospect is simply wishful thinking. To begin with, the Salvadoran government—or the United States—would have to change radically the military leadership of the army. But in favor of whom? The army today, as U.S. diplomats admit, has moved to the right, and is hardly disposed to power-sharing, while the new president, José Napoleón Duarte, does not have the effective authority to compel the army to change its views. Indeed, such an attempt could imperil his own position.

How, then, could the armed forces be persuaded even to entertain the possibility of broad representation in the National Assembly? The American strategy has been to "professionalize" the army, which means changing the nature of the officer corps itself. The American program of training the cadets at Fort Benning is seen as the most effective method of achieving this separation of the officer corps from the intransigent right wing. But even in the unlikely event that this strategy should work and the new armed forces would suppress the death squads and offer increased protection for any of Duarte's so-called left-of-center programs, it will take time. Four to six more years is an optimistic estimate, for this policy assumes the deep intolerance of the officers can somehow be changed by sessions at Fort Benning, and that the younger officers will turn against their superiors.

Meanwhile, the Americans are also trying to produce better soldiers, either by sending advisers, now limited to fifty-five, or by taking whole battalions and training them in Honduras at the Regional Military Training Center. However, even when individual units fight well, such as the U.S.-trained Atlacatl "quick-reaction battalion," the Salvadoran army has had no unified command running down from the commander in chief. Each "sector" tended to work on its own—and many units still flee from any serious engagement—which doesn't make defeating the guerrillas, with their own newfound coordination, any easier. At one time the Americans tried to persuade the Salvadoran army that it should not only take prisoners but also rehabilitate the provinces in which it has been fighting the guerrillas. By repairing the roads, opening the schools and improving health care, the army would demonstrate its concern for the local population. As in Vietnam, the government would aim to win not only the battle against the guerrillas, but also "the hearts and minds" of the people. Unfortunately, that kind of program requires not only many soldiers, but a willingness to encourage them to undertake what amounts to social reform. In fact, few soldiers have been made available for this plan, which one of the ablest commanders feels is "made in America" and not suited to the waging of a successful war.

The military situation remains, at best, a stalemate. The estimated 10,000 to 12,000 guerrillas can move about at will in the eastern sectors and in pockets in the country to the north and east. But when the army arrives in force, the guerrillas scatter, taking their dead with them in order to prevent a body count. The army occupies the territory, leaving the guerrillas to strike again in a different place. Whether the FMLN has any strength in the cities remains an open question; the U.S. military advisers think not. Neither they nor U.S. diplomats claim that the victims of the death squads in the cities are supporters of the FMLN: they are simply people who have been identified, or misidentified, as critical of the right-wing military.

Duarte's election aside, with the continued violation of human rights, U.S. congressional support for the Salvadoran armed forces (which dwindled steadily during the months leading up to the election) is likely to come under ever greater attack at home. The Salvadoran right understands this, but prefers to believe that the Reagan Administration's commitment to prevent a Marxist takeover in their country is so great that it will never abandon the army—and the army will certainly never abandon the Reagan Administration. Meanwhile, the Americans play for time, fulminate against the death squads and threaten the armed forces with a cutback in aid if they don't clean up their behavior.

Some Americans have argued that the United States must make it absolutely clear to both the Duarte government and the Salvadoran army that it will pull out of the country if the killing of civilians is not stopped. Several Salvadorans I talked to made a chilling argument against such an ultimatum: the army, left to itself, might well reenact the massacres of 1932, when up to 30,000 peasants who were thought to have been involved in uprisings against the oligarchs were slaughtered. This may be a fantasy intended precisely to forestall an ultimatum, but there is no guarantee that the army would succumb to American threats, which have proved so hollow in the past.

Without power-sharing, the United States will doubtless go on trying to change the nature of the armed forces until it concludes that this is a futile task —something that the Duarte government's future success (or failure) in controlling the army may finally make clear. Only at that point could we expect that an American withdrawal would be considered, even though this risks an FMLN victory.

Withdrawal of military support would be extremely difficult for any American Administration. In Havana, the Cubans now acknowledge their tutelage of the FMLN, and this should be expected to continue. Notwithstanding the claims by the political spokesmen for the guerrillas, that they seek a democratic solution and will need good relations with the United States, no one can be confident of what would follow a takeover by the FMLN: the result might be as bloody and repressive as the situation is today. The United States could make it clear in advance that any installation of Soviet bases or missiles would not be tolerated, should the Russians be foolish enough to attempt this (and there is no indication that they would). But it would take resourceful economic and political diplomacy to retain U.S. influence in El Salvador.

2

Much of the future debate over what the United States should or should not do in Central America will continue to center around the notion that the United States will lose its "credibility" as a superpower if it cannot hold control there. The credibility argument, as former Assistant Secretary of State for Inter-American Affairs Viron P. Vaky shows in his fine essay in the Carnegie study, easily leads to the conclusion "that the mere *existence* of a Marxist regime in Central America damages U.S. 'credibility' *whether or not* it is linked to Soviet power." If this is so, then of course it is hard to see how we can negotiate security guarantees with Nicaragua's Sandinistas, in which case there will be no choice except to overthrow their regime. If we can't do it with our proxies—the *contras* —and it does not appear that we can, then we may have to use every form of pressure we can devise, from economic starvation to military intimidation. And if these don't work, the logic of the position leads to U.S. intervention. If we cannot get support at home for such a foreign adventure, then, so goes the argument, our "credibility" suffers.

So, too, with El Salvador. If the army does not reform itself, the process of political democratization will most likely go nowhere. We can exhort the military to change; but what if we do not have the means to do so unless we send in our own troops, a not-very-likely prospect under present political conditions? Despite the Kissinger commission's view that military aid must be contingent on significant improvement in human rights, the Salvadoran armed forces may continue to believe they can ignore Washington's pleas because the Administration thinks U.S. "credibility" will be gravely affected if a Marxist state comes into being in El Salvador. In these circumstances, the prospects are, as Vaky puts it, that "the situation will continue along its present course—with continued conflict and bloodshed; increasing American involvement in El Salvador's national life, and growing temptation to become more deeply involved in the military conflict, either directly with advisers and special personnel or through . . . proxies."[14]

So far, the Reagan Administration appears unwilling to contemplate negotiation seriously as a way of accommodating itself to situations that may prove beyond its control. It does not believe it can live with a Marxist-Leninist regime in Nicaragua. But it may have to. It does not believe it can tolerate a takeover by insurgents in El Salvador. But it may have to. Not so long ago, an American Administration was accused by its opponents of having "lost" China to the Communists. A couple of decades later, Washington established relations with China and even saw it as a putative ally in its struggle against the Soviet Union. The opening to China was considered wise by American allies. By abandoning a mistaken policy in Vietnam, the Nixon Administration was perceived as pursuing a mature and productive foreign policy. Similarly, creative diplomatic policies are now required if we are to effectively alter the current situation in Central America.

A U.S. policy likely to have the support of most Latin Americans and able to open up a new era in U.S.– Central American relations would be a policy aimed at the *demilitarization* of the region.

Toward Nicaragua, as I have suggested, this would mean negotiating security guarantees with the Sandinistas that would allay the fears of its neighbors that armed insurrection was being exported from Managua. It would mean curtailing the "covert war" mounted by the *contras* which the United States has been supporting from sanctuaries in neighboring Honduras. Along with the Contadora group and members of the Socialist International (which includes leaders of the Socialist parties in Europe and Latin America), the United States must continue to press the regime for democratic reforms. The strength of the Roman Catholic Church and the continuing pressure from the private sector cannot be underestimated in a country whose economy is a shambles—with per capita income in Nicaragua one third of what it was in 1979. If unhappy Nicaragua becomes a society modeled after Cuba's, dependent on Soviet money to keep its economy from collapse, it will fail, as Cuba has failed, and be a model for no one. But should this happen, Nicaragua's neighbors must perceive it as an internal development, not forced upon Nicaragua by the hostility of the United States. West European governments and interested Latin American governments such as Mexico, Colombia and Venezuela can offer economic incentives for Nicaragua to restore political pluralism; this does not by any means guarantee success in such an undertaking. But if the United States fears for its own security, it must insist that Nicaragua not allow Soviet bases or missiles on its territory.

A policy devised to reduce the Nicaraguan military build-up and eliminate material support for the Salvadoran rebels also requires a demilitarization of Honduras. The construction, as now planned, of long-term U.S. bases in Honduras must therefore be discontinued. The presence of thousands of U.S. troops on maneuvers greatly strengthens the military in a country whose democracy is fragile.[15] While the election for president in 1981 was democratic by any standard, the militarization of Honduras by the United States has put the armed forces in a commanding position inside the country. And by casting the problems of this wretchedly poor nation in East-West terms, the United States has helped to put aside any talk of economic reform. However, General Walter López Reyes, the commander of the Honduran armed forces, who replaced General Alvarez, called for new limits to military spending and a new search for peaceful solutions for the region.[16] What Honduras needs is not more American money for military purposes (which has already risen from $11 billion in 1982 to a scheduled $40 billion in 1984), but a renegotiation of its national debt.

For the United States, the choices it faces in El Salvador are less clear. The government in Nicaragua is a functioning government with which Washington can negotiate—*if* it chooses to. No matter how the elections of November 1984 are organized inside Nicaragua, it will be a Sandinista who rules in Managua. In Honduras, there is a democratic structure that can be strengthened, just as there are security guarantees that can be concluded between Tegucigalpa and Managua. In El Salvador, however, the presidential election has bought only time. It is hard to see how the military can be brought under effective civilian control, when this would have to mean the removal of much of the upper ranks of the officer corps. Even with a Christian Democrat as president, the legislative assembly remains under the control of the rightist parties; the officers operating the death squads are still closely connected to the highest-ranking officers in the armed forces, and the current minister of defense, General Vides Casanova, who was chief of the National Guard when the four American churchwomen were killed in 1980, was kept on by the new president.[17]

Under these conditions, the United States will have to set a time limit—perhaps six months after the election—to see if the new government can effectively control the armed forces, which means the elimination of the death squads and the imprisonment or exile of those officers who were implicated in the killings. Simply transferring officers to other posts within the country—or even abroad—will not be enough; the Salvadoran military will have to be radically reconstituted if there is to be any hope for a democratic tendency to take hold in El Salvador.

By getting rid of extremists in the military, the new

president might be able to initiate talks with the rebels and then progressively isolate the most radical groups. The only power-sharing arrangement that might possibly succeed would be one that exploits the divisions on the left. But this is a highly optimistic scenario. Most likely, the war will go on, the death squads will remain active and support for the rebels will grow. At best, a U.S. timetable for withdrawal of economic and military aid can be a last opportunity to put pressure on the government in San Salvador to act—which means, in effect, to force the military to purge itself.

If the armed forces refuse to take measures such as these that might yield some reasonable hope of ending the conflict, then the United States must draw the necessary conclusions and act on them. As McGeorge Bundy, special assistant for national security affairs to Presidents Kennedy and Johnson, has written, deliberately drawing a lesson from Vietnam, if the Salvadoran government "acts in a way that makes it impossible for our help to be effective, and if we either will not or cannot persuade it to change its ways, then the sooner we get out the better."[18] But what of the possibility I have already mentioned, that, faced with unilateral U.S. withdrawal, the Salvadoran armed forces may massacre large numbers of their nation's population, using widespread, indiscriminate terror to keep themselves in power?

As the case of present-day Guatemala demonstrates vividly, faced with such a situation there is comparatively little we can do. If the leaders of any nation are willing to use mass murder, extortion and torture as instruments of national policy, and other countries are unwilling or unable to intervene directly in the affairs of that nation, then few choices are left. We can attempt to apply varying degrees of pressure by cutting aid and reducing our commercial involvement, or we can go the full course and treat such countries as "pariah nations," withholding any and all support and urging our allies to do likewise. There is, of course, no guarantee that this will alter the behavior of the country in question—but *no* policy can supply such a guarantee, except perhaps unilateral military intervention, which is something that the United States, given not only its experience in Vietnam but the history of its involvement in Central America as well, should—and does—view with great wariness.

Disengagement from El Salvador, however, does not mean the United States should be indifferent to what takes place in the region. We made it clear to the Russians twenty years ago that we would not tolerate missiles deployed on Cuban soil; we can make it known again that we will not tolerate any introduction of Soviet nuclear weapons into Central America. But we have also been concerned with stability—and the country that should most concern us is Mexico. Indeed, the final argument the Reagan Administration has used to justify its military build-up in Central America is that such action is a hedge against the spread of leftist revolutions to Mexico, the so-called last domino.

While Mexico has shown remarkable resiliency over the past half-century, the problems it now faces are grave. It is certainly in the interest of the United States that Mexico maintain its stability—but the place to look for trouble is not in neighboring Central America but in Mexico itself. What may threaten Mexico in the near future, as it does Brazil, Argentina and, in Central America, Costa Rica, are the enormous debt-servicing charges that have come due after the profligate spending such countries indulged in during the 1970s. Mexico, for instance, because of the new sources of oil that it had discovered, felt secure enough to apply for enormous loans overseas, and banks were only too happy to lend. Growth was high and prospects looked good for the Mexican economy until the price of oil dropped in the 1980s. At that point it became evident that Mexico had borrowed against a limitless future and was going to be hard put to fulfill its financial obligations; the peso lost 80 percent of its value in 1982, and Mexico found itself unable to make the repayments due on its government debt. As a result, the Mexican government agreed in August 1982 to institute an austerity program, borrowed funds from international lending organizations and had the private banks reschedule the principal of its debt.

But the problem is far from solved. Mexico's economy has declined sharply. Unemployment has risen. Inflation in 1983 was running at over 90 percent. Since the United States is a major lender, its interest rates affect any further Latin American borrowings; with U.S. deficits of $200 billion to $300 billion projected well into the future, these interest rates are likely to stay high. It will be nigh impossible for Mexico to meet interest payments over the next few years without instituting socially dangerous austerity programs, when (as of 1983) it owes $89 billion to Western and Japanese banks and has to use approximately 50 percent of its export earnings to service this debt.[19] While Mexico has so far been able to earn the hard currency to pay the interest rates on its debt, this has been at the cost of a 70 percent fall in imports. Mexico is therefore in a situation where its main export revenue from oil is being used to service its debt, while its social problems pile up dangerously. Should United States interest rates rise, a sharp increase in debt-servicing costs could quickly destroy any progress that has already been achieved.

What is to be done? Here is a nation whose capital city is expected, by the year 2000, to have a population of 30 million, and is in danger of losing its water supply. If Mexico is even to begin to cope with this ballooning population (one to two million Mexicans now enter the United States illegally each year) and to create the 700,000 jobs a year it will need, its debt will have to be restructured. There are a number of ways this can be accomplished, all of which are applicable not only to Mexico but to other troubled Latin nations, and all of which have important implications for the government and the citizens of the United States.

First, we can forgive the debts that the Mexican government owes to our government. Such a move would provide Mexico with immediate (though partial) economic relief and an increased capability to cope with its other obligations—but what effect would it have on the United States? On the most obvious level, it would lead to an increase in the federal budget deficit and would thus hinder efforts to keep interest rates low. Of even greater concern would be the question of how other debtor governments would view such an act. If the United States were to forgive the Mexican debt, nations such as Brazil and Argentina would naturally seek a similar arrangement—and since it would not be economically feasible for our country to forgive *all* debts, we would have to devise criteria to determine which, if any, additional debts would be forgiven and which would not. But criteria based on what? Importance to our national security, or to our business community? Willingness to assist in attaining U.S. goals in the hemisphere? Record on human rights? Under this scenario, forgiving debts comes dangerously close to a punishment-and-reward system, never a sound basis for the conduct of foreign relations. Because of this, and because of the effects it would have on the U.S. budget, forgiving debt is neither a realistic nor a desirable policy alternative.

A second possibility for the U.S. government would be to change Federal Reserve regulations so that U.S. banks can agree to a postponement of the interest payments without having to write off Latin American obligations as bad debts. As it is now, the nine largest U.S. banks, with total capital of $27 billion, have lent more than $30 billion (or more than their net worth) to private and governmental borrowers in just three countries: Mexico, Brazil and Argentina. (It is important to note that, in addition to their own resources, these larger banks often use funds representing the assets of a network of smaller regional banks located throughout the United States.) Were any of these countries to find themselves unable to keep up their interest payments, under U.S. law the debts involved would have to be listed as "nonperforming loans"— the banks' profits would be reduced, which would cause stockholders to take serious losses.

In addition, significant amounts of the banks' assets would become liabilities, which would be likely to trigger a rise in U.S. interest rates as the banks themselves attempted to recoup losses. Thus the ability of Latin American debtor nations to pay back their loans has important implications for all Americans, not simply banking executives or large-scale investors— indeed, in a "worst-possible" default situation, the United States might see some of its hardest-hit banks fail outright. This, too, would have a profound effect on the American public; though many depositors would be covered by federal insurance, the cost of restoring funds to citizens whose banks had failed could only cause yet another increase in the federal deficit, which would, in turn, result in a further rise in interest rates. But by changing Federal Reserve regulations to allow American banks a longer period of time before declaring their Latin loans to be in default, the U.S. government might avert such admittedly disastrous events.

Additional time to restructure the interest rates on loans due, however, will *not* help the further and more serious plight of Latin America's debtor nations— their inability to earn enough foreign currency to allow them both to expand their economies and to bear the burden of even reduced interest payments. It is not simply a question of receiving new loans in order to keep up interest payments but of needing a real transfer of resources, so that they actually take in more cash than they pay out. We must adopt programs that will help to ensure that, at the end of these periods of grace, the Latin nations will have a better chance of coping with their debts than they do now. Otherwise, we merely prolong the inevitable; given their present structure, the debts of Latin America cannot be repaid, either now or in the future. But these debts can be restructured. Felix Rohatyn, the New York–based financial expert, has suggested that the short-term, high-interest loans extended to Latin America be replaced by long-term loans with low interest. A new agency would have to be created for this purpose, one that would acquire the banks' credits in exchange for long-term, low-interest bonds of its own. Similar restructuring schemes have been advanced by other experts, but the point of all of them is clear— solving the debt problem is only a preliminary measure to the creation of economic stability, not vice versa. As Rohatyn puts it, "It is not enough to say that economic recovery will solve this problem [since] we may never get recovery unless we solve the problem first."[20]

There are other methods available to us that might further help the Latin American nations gain greater control of their debt situation. One of these (and one that was virtually ignored by the Kissinger commission) is a reconstruction of present trade arrangements. The Latin American nations have a long tradition of heavy reliance on mutual, or intraregional, trade, a tradition that was born out of their once expansive markets and healthy economies. But recent developments have transformed intraregional trade from a boon into a curse. Whereas it was once practical, even healthy, for the Latin nations to do upwards of 25 percent of their trading with each other, now, with most of their economies in turmoil, the process has become one of simply moving goods and funds from one insolvent nation to another. Without increased exports to other regions, notably the West and Japan, it will be impossible for Latin America's economy to recover.

But how is this to be accomplished when, as political economist Jeffrey Garten has pointed out, "the markets of the West and Japan may have great difficulty accepting a major surge of Latin goods?"[21] There are solutions available, though they will admittedly be difficult to implement because of domestic policies both at home and abroad. Garten suggests that the United States, in return for allowing Latin America to export more of its goods to this country, should itself receive concessions from the nations of the region, including "greater market access for our service industries, such as computer and insurance companies." Some American producers, despite these concessions, would almost certainly be injured by the liberalization of U.S. trade barriers with regard to Latin America— but, as Garten says, "better to compensate those American producers . . . than to put the money directly into Central America."[22] Such trade programs would have to be conducted with great care, and would be likely to take time; patience on the part of both the United States and the Latin American region would be essential.

In addition to trade programs, there is the perennial question of direct U.S. aid. Doubtless, such aid can assist the Latin debtors to apply their national profits to pay back their loans. But we must be cautious— there is a point at which direct aid no longer has a bearing on the debt question. If too much aid is pumped directly into these countries, much of it can and does end up in places for which it was not designed, private pockets being chief among them. Only as much aid as can be quickly and demonstrably absorbed should be provided.

The task for the United States, then, is to deal with the very real social and economic problems of Mexico and the other Latin American debtor nations without tying the solutions to the ideological thrust of Central America's revolutions. What Mexico fears is not Marxism-Leninism in El Salvador or Nicaragua but the risk of a widening war. In any such generalized conflict in the region, Mexico might well be dragged in. As Carlos Fuentes points out, "Mexico would be under tremendous pressure to come down on the side of the U.S. in a war, not to appear as harboring revolutionaries or in any way sympathizing with forces that will then be presented as outright enemies of the U.S. ... [But] if Mexico comes down on the side of the U.S. openly in a situation of generalized conflict, it will lose its nationalist consensus and legitimacy and provoke an onslaught from the left." On the other hand, were Mexico to come down on the side of Managua—and by extension Cuba, and by further extension the Soviet Union—there would be pressure from the United States and the right wing in Mexico. The delicate balance between the left and the right would be broken, and Mexico would be destabilized. Ironically, the United States "would play the role of the domino pusher from the North." This, Fuentes warns, "would be the ultimate accomplishment of Washington's penchant for self-fulfilling prophecy: a Mexico destabilized by American nightmares about Mexico."[23]

If, however, the United States were to adopt a policy of allowing Mexico to join with the other Contadora countries and take the lead in finding peaceful solutions for the region—and this is the way to encourage Mexico not to return to its isolationist past—Washington could devote its considerable diplomatic and financial resources to working with Mexico and Costa Rica to solve their debt problems. After all, stability in the region is as much in Mexico's interest as it is in America's. Today, the spillover of refugees from the activities of the Guatemalan guerrillas threatens Mexico's southern provinces, and Mexico is worried about the unrest among its own Indians that this might stir up. But it is important to understand that if Marxist rebels in Guatemala were able to install a leftist government in Guatemala City in the not too distant future, the first thing they would ask for, as a high Mexican official has suggested, would be a nonaggression pact with Mexico. Fuentes is right to note that it would be the United States, not a small

Central American state, that would be the domino pusher if Mexico were to become destabilized because of external revolution in the region.

In confronting the probability of continuing turmoil in Central America over the next decade, the United States must finally learn to distinguish between indigenous revolution and Soviet-inspired subversion. It must do more than accept change only in order that things remain the same, that is to say, maintaining U.S. predominance in the region. It must seek to create stability out of revolution rather than fear revolution and, in so doing, work with revolutionary governments to prevent their alignment with and dependence on the Soviet Union. The U.S.-Soviet rivalry in the Third World will very likely be played out in the Western Hemisphere, with Latin America's huge debts and unstable regimes. It will be a test of our maturity to demonstrate that we can understand the difference between trying to create democracy in a barren setting and reinforcing democracy where it already exists. We misread history if we conclude that democracy is impossible in Central America. Again and again when it has been snuffed out, it reappears —in 1948 in Costa Rica, in the 1950s in Guatemala, in 1972 in El Salvador, in 1979 in Nicaragua, in 1981 in Honduras.

Today America's "credibility" is indeed in question because of the obtuseness of her foreign policy. By continuing a long history of relying on repressive local military forces to maintain stability in Central America, the United States does not appear to be planning for a future that will allow countries with fragile democracies to grow stronger and hardy democracies to flourish. If it were to concentrate on negotiating security guarantees for the region rather than on arming it, then the United States might find that its credibility was in fact improved, because countries both friendly and unfriendly would recognize that Washington was at last acting with good sense. The exercise of American power should derive from an unblinkered assessment of American interests. To the extent that America is found wanting in this respect, her alliances will suffer and her enemies rejoice.

NOTES

PART ONE

1. New York *Times,* February 9, 1984, p. 19.

2. Source: New York *Times,* March 11, 1984.

3. Frederick Merk, *Manifest Destiny and Mission in American History* (New York: Knopf, 1963), p. 9.

4. Walter LaFeber, *Inevitable Revolutions* (New York: Norton, 1983), p. 22.

5. *Ibid.,* p. 23.

6. Ernest May, *The American Foreign Policy* (New York: Braziller, 1963), p. 63.

7. LaFeber, *op. cit.,* p. 19.

8. Merk, *op. cit.,* p. 16.

9. *Ibid.,* p. 17.

10. Ernest May, *The Making of the Monroe Doctrine* (Cambridge, Massachusetts: Harvard University Press, Belknap Press, 1975), pp. 130–131.

11. Henry Stimson, *American Policy in Nicaragua* (New York: Scribner's, 1927), p. 10.

12. Kenneth Bourne, *Britain and the Balance of Power in North America* (Berkeley, California: University of California Press, 1967), p. 178.

13. *Ibid.,* p. 182.

14. *Ibid.,* p. 202.

15. Samuel Eliot Morison and Henry Steele Commager, *The Growth of the American Republic, 1865–1937* (New York: Oxford, 1940), p. 320.

16. LaFeber, *op. cit.,* p. 33.

17. *Ibid.,* p. 37.

18. *Ibid.,* p. 38.

19. Samuel Eliot Morison, Frederick Merk and Frank Freidel, *Dissent in Three American Wars* (Cambridge, Massachusetts: Harvard University Press, 1970), p. 72.

20. *Ibid.,* p. 90.

21. *Ibid.,* p. 95.

22. May, *The American Foreign Policy,* p. 145.

23. *Ibid.,* p. 143.

24. See Samuel Flagg Bemis in Edward Buehrig, *Wilson's Foreign Policy in Perspective* (Bloomington, Indiana: Indiana University Press, 1957), p. 115.

25. LaFeber, *op. cit.,* p. 53.

26. *Ibid.,* p. 51.

27. *Ibid.*

28. See Richard L. Millett, Manchester *Guardian,* August 28, 1983.

29. LaFeber, *op. cit.,* p. 66.

30. Eduardo Crawley, *Dictators Never Die* (New York: St. Martin's, 1979).

31. *Time,* November 15, 1948, p. 43.

32. Edward G. Miller, "Nonintervention and Collective Responsibility in the Americas," *Department of State Bulletin* 23 (May 15, 1950), pp. 768–770.

33. LaFeber, *op. cit.,* p. 107.

34. *Ibid.*

35. *Nomination of John Foster Dulles,* U.S. Congress, Senate Committee on Foreign Relations, 83rd Congress, 1st Session, 1953, p. 31.

36. *Statements of Secretary John Foster Dulles and Admiral Arthur Radford,* U.S. Congress, Senate Committee on Foreign Relations, 83rd Congress, 2nd Session, March 9 and April 14, 1954, p. 18.

37. Stephen Schlesinger and Stephen Kinzer, *Bitter Fruit* (New York: Doubleday, 1982).

38. *Ibid.*

39. Theodore C. Sorensen, *Kennedy* (New York: Harper & Row, 1965), p. 535.

40. See Oral History Interview, Harry McPherson, Tape no. 4, 13, Lyndon B. Johnson Library, cited in LaFeber, *op. cit.*, p. 318.

41. LaFeber, *op cit.*, p. 156.

42. *Ibid.*, p. 202.

43. *Ibid.*, p. 205.

44. Ibid, p. 269.

PART TWO

1. New York *Times*, July 28, 1983.

2. Nestor D. Sanchez, "The Communist Threat," *Foreign Policy*, Fall 1983.

3. See the testimony of Arturo J. Cruz, who was a member of the government junta from April 1980 to March 1981 and subsequently left Nicaragua, convinced that the Sandinistas were betraying the "democratic and pluralistic ideals" of the revolution; in "Nicaragua's Imperiled Revolution," *Foreign Affairs*, Summer 1983.

4. New York *Times*, July 18, 1983.

5. New York *Times*, July 26 and July 30, 1983.

6. New York *Times*, July 20 and July 30, 1983.

7. See James Chace, "Getting Out of the Central American Maze," *New York Review of Books*, June 24, 1982.

8. See James Chace, "The Endless War," *New York Review of Books*, December 8, 1983.

9. New York *Times*, November 27 and December 4, 1983.

10. Fred Iklé, Under Secretary of Defense for Policy, was deeply skeptical of Managua's concessions. "It is in their inter-

est to go through the motions of negotiating," he said. "Can they be trusted to abide by an agreement? Probably not." Quoted in the *Wall Street Journal,* December 30, 1983.

11. A comprehensive and highly classified analysis of the Salvadoran military along these lines was prepared by Brigadier General Frederick F. Woerner, Jr., who is based at the U.S. Southern Command in Panama; his conclusions were reaffirmed two years later in conversations with a visiting congressional delegation. See the New York *Times,* April 22, 1983.

12. New York *Times,* November 3, 1983.

13. New York *Times,* January 8, 1984.

14. New York *Times,* March 3, 1984.

15. New York *Times,* February 1, 1984.

16. See the Rockefeller Report on Latin America, *Hearing before the Subcommittee on Western Hemisphere Affairs of the Committee on Foreign Relations,* United States Senate, 91st Congress, November 20, 1969 (Washington: GPO, 1970), p. 86. "In short, a new type of military man is coming to the fore and often becoming a major force for constructive social change in the American republics. Motivated by increasing impatience with corruption, inefficiency, and a stagnant political order, the new military man is prepared to adapt his authoritarian tradition to the goals of social and economic progress."

17. All quotes taken from *The Report of the President's National Bipartisan Commission on Central America* (New York: Macmillan, 1984).

18. Theodore Moran, "The Cost of Alternative U.S. Policies toward El Salvador," in Robert S. Leiken, ed., *Central America: Anatomy of a Conflict* (Elmsford, N.Y.: Pergamon Press–Carnegie Endowment for International Peace, 1984).

19. All quotes *ibid.*

20. See Chace, "The Endless War."

21. See the report by Stephen Kinzer, New York *Times*, January 29, 1984.

22. Washington *Post*, January 29, 1984.

PART THREE

1. See James Chace, "Getting Out of the Central American Maze," *New York Review of Books*, June 24, 1982.

2. New York *Times*, February 28, 1984.

3. Text in Spanish published in *Granma* (Havana), October 7, 1983.

4. Figures from the U.S. Department of State, Bureau of Public Affairs, "Background Notes: Cuba," April 1983.

5. Castro speech, broadcast in Spanish, Havana Domestic Service, July 26, 1983—FBIS.

6. New York *Times*, October 28, 1983.

7. See Seweryn Bialer and Alfred Stepan, "Cuba, the U.S. and the Central American Mess," *New York Review of Books*, May 27, 1982.

8. See the report in the *Sunday Times* of London, October 23, 1983.

9. New York *Times*, February 24, 1984.

10. New York *Times*, February 2, 1984.

11. New York *Times*, February 10, 1984.

12. See the report in the *Sunday Times* of London, October 30, 1983.

13. For the argument in favor of power-sharing, see Piero Gleijes, "The Case for Power Sharing in El Salvador," *Foreign Affairs*, Summer 1983. See also Robert W. Tucker, "Their Wars, Our Choices," *New Republic*, October 24, 1983.

14. Viron Vaky, "Reagan's Central American Policy: An Isthmus Restored," in Leiken, ed., *op. cit.*

15. New York *Times*, February 24, 1984.

16. See "Honduras: Democracy in Demise," published by the Washington Office on Latin America, February 1984; see also the New York *Times,* June 7, 1984.

17. New York *Times,* March 4, 1984.

18. McGeorge Bundy's letter in *Foreign Affairs,* Fall 1983.

19. Sources: World Bank; American Express Bank; U.N. Economic Commission for Latin America; Wharton Economic Forecasting—in the New York *Times,* Section F, p. 1, March 11, 1984.

20. Felix Rohatyn, *The Twenty-Year Century* (New York: Random House, 1983), Chapter Two. See also Jeffrey E. Garten, "The Big Debtors Try to Dig Themselves Out," *Wall Street Journal,* August 1, 1983.

21. Garten, *op. cit.*

22. Jeffrey E. Garten, "Aid in the Eighties," *New York Times Magazine,* March 25, 1984.

23. Interview with Carlos Fuentes in *New Perspectives,* Vol. I, No. 1, Winter 1983–84 (Institute for National Strategy, Los Angeles, California).